American Buffalo

AmericanBuffalo
loAmericanBuffal
aloAmericanBuff
ffaloAmericanBu
uffaloAmericanB
BuffaloAmerican
nBuffaloAmerica
anBuffaloAmeric
icanBuffaloAmeri
ricanBuffaloAme
ericanBuffaloAm
mericanBuffaloA

AmericanBuffalo

a play by David Mamet

Grove Press, Inc., New York

First Evergreen Edition 1977
First Printing 1977
ISBN: 0-394-17016-4
Grove Press ISBN: 0-8021-4099-8
Library of Congress Catalog Card Number: 77-78079

Manufactured in the United States of America

Distributed by Random House, Inc., New York

GROVE PRESS, INC.
196 West Houston Street, New York, N.Y. 10014

This play is dedicated to Mr. J. J. Johnston of Chicago, Illinois.

American Buffalo was first produced by the Goodman Theatre Stage Two, Chicago, Illinois, and opened on November 23, 1975, with the following cast:

BOBBY	William H. Macy
TEACH	Bernard Erhard
DONNY	J. J. Johnston

This production was directed by Gregory Mosher; set by Michael Merritt; lighting by Robert Christen.

After a twelve-performance showcase at Stage Two, it re-opened at Chicago's St. Nicholas Theatre Company, with Mike Nussbaum in the role of TEACH.

In February, 1976, it was showcased at St. Clement's, New York, with the following cast:

BOBBY	J. T. Walsh
TEACH	Mike Kellin
DONNY	Michael Egan

This production was directed by Gregory Mosher; set by Akira Yoshimura; lighting by Gary Porto.

The New York Broadway production at the Ethel Barrymore Theatre opened on February 16, 1977, with the following cast:

BOBBY	John Savage
TEACH	Robert Duvall
DONNY	Kenneth McMillan

This production was directed by Ulu Grosbard; set by Santo Loquasto; lighting by Jules Fisher.

"Mine eyes have seen the glory of the coming of the Lord.
He is peeling down the alley in a black and yellow Ford."

Folk Tune.

THE CHARACTERS

DON DUBROW   A man in his late forties, the owner of
                    Don's Resale Shop

WALTER COLE
called TEACH   A friend and associate of Don

BOB   Don's gopher

THE SCENE

Don's Resale Shop. A junkshop.

THE TIME

One Friday. Act One takes place in the morning; Act Two
starts around 11:00 that night.

ACT I

Don's Resale Shop. Morning. DON *and* BOB *are sitting.*

DON: So?

> *Pause.*

So what, Bob?

> *Pause.*

BOB: I'm sorry, Donny.

> *Pause.*

DON: All right.

BOB: I'm sorry, Donny.

> *Pause.*

DON: Yeah.

BOB: Maybe he's still in there.

DON: If you think that, Bob, how come you're here?

BOB: I came in.

> *Pause.*

DON: You don't come in, Bob. You don't come in until you do a thing.

BOB: He didn't come out.

DON: What do I care, Bob, if he came out or not? You're s'posed to watch the guy, you watch him. Am I wrong?

BOB: I just went to the back.

DON: Why?

> *Pause.*

Why did you do that?

BOB: 'Cause he wasn't coming out the front.

DON: Well, Bob, I'm sorry, but this isn't good enough. If you want to do business . . . if we got a business deal, it isn't good enough. I want you to remember this.

BOB: I do.

DON: Yeah, *now* . . . but later, what?

> *Pause.*

> Just one thing, Bob. Action counts.

> *Pause.*

> Action talks and bullshit walks.

BOB: I only went around to see he's coming out the back.

DON: No, don't go fuck yourself around with these excuses.

> *Pause.*

BOB: I'm sorry.

DON: Don't tell me that you're sorry. I'm not mad at you.

BOB: You're not?

DON *(Pause)*: Let's clean up here.

> BOB *starts to clean up the debris around the poker table.*

> The only thing I'm trying to teach you something here.

BOB: Okay.

DON: Now lookit Fletcher.

BOB: Fletch?

DON: Now, Fletcher is a standup guy.

BOB: Yeah.

DON: I don't *give* a shit. He is a fellow stands for something—

BOB: Yeah.

DON: You take him and you put him down in some strange town with just a nickel in his pocket, and by nightfall he'll have that town by the balls. This is not talk, Bob, this is action.

> *Pause.*

BOB: He's a real good card player.

DON: You're fucking A he is, Bob, and this is what I'm getting at. Skill. Skill and talent and the balls to arrive at your own *conclusions.*

The fucker won four hundred bucks last night.

BOB: Yeah?

DON: *Oh* yeah.

BOB: And who was playing?

DON: *Me* . . .

BOB: Uh-huh . . .

DON: And *Teach* . . .

BOB: (How'd Teach do?)*

DON: (Not too good.)

BOB: (No, huh?)

DON: (No.) . . . and Earl was here . . .

BOB: Uh-huh . . .

DON: And Fletcher.

BOB: *How'd* he do?

DON: He won four hundred bucks.

BOB: And who else won?

DON: Ruthie, she won.

BOB: She won, huh?

DON: Yeah.

BOB: She does okay.

DON: *Oh* yeah . . .

BOB: She's an okay card player.

DON: Yes, she is.

BOB: I like her.

DON: Fuck, I like her, too. (There's nothing wrong in that.)

---

* Some portions of the dialogue appear in parentheses, which serve to mark a slight change of outlook on the part of the speaker—perhaps a momentary change to a more introspective regard. —D.M.

BOB: (No.)

DON: I mean, she treats you right.

BOB: Uh-huh. How'd she do?

DON: She did okay.

   Pause.

BOB: You win?

DON: I did all right.

BOB: Yeah?

DON: Yeah. I did okay. Not like *Fletch* . . .

BOB: No, huh?

DON: I mean, Fletcher, he plays *cards*.

BOB: He's real sharp.

DON: You're goddamn right he is.

BOB: I know it.

DON: Was he born that way?

BOB: Huh?

DON: I'm saying was he born that way or do you think he had to learn it?

BOB: Learn it.

DON: Goddamn right he did, and don't forget it.

   Everything, Bobby: it's going to happen to you, it's *not* going to happen to you, the important thing is can you deal with it, and can you *learn* from it.

   Pause.

   And this is why I'm telling you to stand up. It's no different with you than with anyone else. Everything that I or Fletcher know we picked up on the street. That's all business is . . . common sense, experience, and talent.

BOB: Like when he jewed Ruthie out that pig iron.

DON: What pig iron?

BOB: That he got off her that time.

DON: When was this?

BOB: On the back of her truck.

DON: That wasn't, I don't think, her pig iron.

BOB: No?

DON: That was *his* pig iron, Bob.

BOB: Yeah?

DON: Yeah. He bought it off her.

    Pause.

BOB: Well, she was real mad at him.

DON: She was.

BOB: Yup.

DON: She was mad at him?

BOB: Yeah. That he stole her pig iron.

DON: He didn't steal it, Bob.

BOB: No?

DON: No.

BOB: She was *mad* at him . . .

DON: Well, that very well may be, Bob, but the fact remains that it was *business*. That's what business *is*.

BOB: What?

DON: People taking *care* of themselves. Huh?

BOB: No.

DON: 'Cause there's business and there's friendship, Bobby . . . there are many things, and when you walk around you *hear* a lot of things, and what you got to do is keep clear who your friends are, and who treated you like what. Or else the rest is garbage, Bob, because I want to tell you something.

BOB: Okay.

DON: Things are not always what they seem to be.

BOB: I know.

Pause.

DON: There's lotsa people on this street, Bob, they want this and they want that. Do anything to get it. You don't have *friends* this life. . . . You want some breakfast?

BOB: I'm not hungry.

Pause.

DON: *Never* skip breakfast, Bob.

BOB: Why?

DON: Breakfast . . . is the most important meal of the day.

BOB: I'm not hungry.

DON: It makes no earthly difference in the world. You know how much nutritive benefits they got in coffee? Zero. Not one thing. The stuff eats *you* up. You can't live on coffee, Bobby. (And I've told you this before.) You cannot live on cigarettes. You may feel *good*, you may feel *fine*, but something's getting overworked, and you are going to pay for it.

Now: What do you see me eat when I come in here every day?

BOB: Coffee.

DON: Come on, Bob, don't fuck with me. I *drink* a little coffee . . . but what do I *eat*?

BOB: Yogurt.

DON: Why?

BOB: Because it's good for you.

DON: You're goddamn right. And it wouldn't kill you to take a vitamin.

BOB: They're too expensive.

DON: Don't worry about it. You should just take 'em.

BOB: I can't afford 'em.

DON: Don't worry about it.

BOB: You'll buy some for me?

DON: Do you need 'em?

BOB: *Yeah.*

DON: Well, then, I'll get you some. What do you *think?*

BOB: Thanks, Donny.

DON: It's for your own good. Don't thank *me* . . .

BOB: Okay.

DON: I just can't use you in here like a zombie.

BOB: I just went around the back.

DON: I don't care. Do you see? Do you see what I'm getting at?

    Pause.

BOB: Yeah.

    Pause.

DON: Well, we'll see.

BOB: I'm sorry, Donny.

DON: Well, we'll see.

TEACH *(appears in the doorway and enters the store)*: Good morning.

BOB: Morning, Teach.

TEACH *(walks around the store a bit in silence)*: Fuckin' Ruthie, fuckin' Ruthie, fuckin' Ruthie, fuckin' Ruthie, fuckin' Ruthie.

DON: What?

TEACH: Fuckin' *Ruthie* . . .

DON: . . . yeah?

TEACH: I come into the Riverside to get a cup of *coffee,* right? I sit down at the table Grace and Ruthie.

DON: Yeah.

TEACH: I'm gonna order just a cup of coffee.

DON: Right.

TEACH: So Grace and Ruthie's having breakfast, and they're done. *Plates . . . crusts* of stuff all over . . . So we'll shoot the shit.

DON: Yeah.

TEACH: Talk about the *game . . .*

DON: . . . yeah.

TEACH: . . . *so* on. Down I sit. "Hi, hi." I take a piece of toast off Grace's plate . . .

DON: . . . uh-huh . . .

TEACH: : . . and she goes "Help yourself."

Help myself.

I should help myself to half a piece of toast it's four slices for a quarter. I should have a nickel every time we're over at the game, I pop for coffee . . . cigarettes . . . a *sweet roll,* never say word.

"Bobby, see who wants what." Huh? A fucking *roast-beef* sandwich. *(To* BOB*)* Am I right? *(To* DON *)* Ahh, shit. We're sitting down, how many times do I pick up the check? But (No!) because I never go and make a big *thing* out of it—it's no big thing—and flaunt like "This one's on me" like some bust-out asshole, but I naturally assume that I'm with friends, and don't forget who's who when someone gets *behind* a half a yard or needs some help with (huh?) some fucking rent, or drops enormous piles of money at the track, or someone's *sick* or something . . .

DON *(to* BOB*)*: This is what I'm talking about.

TEACH: Only (and I tell you this, Don). Only, and I'm not, I don't think, casting anything on anyone: from the mouth of a Southern bulldyke asshole ingrate of a vicious nowhere cunt can this trash come. *(To* BOB*)* And I take nothing back, and I know you're close with them.

BOB: With Grace and Ruthie?

TEACH: Yes.

BOB: (I like 'em.)

TEACH: I have always treated everybody more than fair, and never gone around complaining. Is this true, Don?

DON: Yup.

TEACH: Someone is *against* me, that's their problem . . . I can look out for myself, and I don't got to fuck around behind somebody's back, I don't like the way they're treating me. (Or pray some brick *safe* falls and hits them on the head, they're walking down the street.)

But to have that shithead turn, in one breath, every fucking sweet roll that I ever ate with them into *ground glass* (I'm wondering were they eating it and thinking "This guy's an idiot to blow a fucking *quarter* on his friends" . . .)

. . . this hurts me, Don.

This hurts me in a way I don't know what the fuck to do.

Pause.

DON: You're probably just upset.

TEACH: You're fuckin' A I'm upset. I am *very* upset, Don.

DON: They got their problems, too, Teach.

TEACH: *I* would like to have their problems.

DON: All I'm saying, nothing *personal* . . . they were probably, uh, *talking* about something.

TEACH: Then let them talk about it, then. No, I am sorry, Don, I cannot brush this off. They treat me like an asshole, they are an asshole.

Pause.

The only way to teach these people is to kill them.

Pause.

DON: You want some coffee?

TEACH: I'm not hungry.

DON: Come on, I'm sending Bobby to the Riverside.

TEACH: (Fuckin' joint . . .)

DON: Yeah.

TEACH: (They harbor *assholes* in there . . .)

DON: Yeah. Come on, Teach, what do you want? Bob?

BOB: Yeah?

DON *(to* TEACH*):* Come on, he's going anyway. *(To* BOB, *handing him a bill)* Get me a Boston, and go for the yogurt.

BOB: What kind?

DON: You know, plain, and, if they don't got it, uh, something else. And get something for yourself.

BOB: What?

DON: Whatever you want. But get something to *eat,* and whatever you want to drink, and get Teacher a coffee.

BOB: Boston, Teach?

TEACH: No.

BOB: What?

TEACH: Black.

BOB: Right.

DON: And something for yourself to eat. *(To* TEACH*)* He doesn't want to eat.

TEACH *(to* BOB*):* You got to eat (And this is what I'm saying at The Riverside.)

     Pause.

BOB: (Black coffee.)

DON: And get something for yourself to eat. *(To* TEACH*)* What do you want to eat? An English muffin? *(To* BOB*)* Get Teach an English muffin.

TEACH: I don't want an English muffin.

DON: Get him an English muffin, and make sure they give you jelly.

TEACH: I don't want an English muffin.

DON: What do you want?

TEACH: I don't want anything.

BOB: Come on, Teach, eat something.

> *Pause.*

DON: You'll feel better you eat something, Teach.

> *Pause.*

TEACH *(to* BOB*)*: Tell 'em to give you an order of bacon, real dry, real crisp.

BOB: Okay.

TEACH: And tell the broad if it's for me she'll give you more.

BOB: Okay.

DON: Anything else you want?

TEACH: No.

DON: A cantaloupe?

TEACH: I never eat cantaloupe.

DON: No?

TEACH: It gives me the runs.

DON: Yeah?

TEACH: And tell him he shouldn't say anything to Ruthie.

DON: He wouldn't.

TEACH: No? No, you're right. I'm sorry, Bob.

BOB: It's okay.

TEACH: I'm upset.

BOB: It's okay, Teach.

> *Pause.*

TEACH: Thank you.

BOB: You're welcome.

> BOB *starts to exit.*

DON: And the plain if they got it.

BOB: I will. *(Exits.)*

DON: He wouldn't say anything.

TEACH: What the fuck do *I* care . . .

> *Pause.*

Cunt.

> *Pause.*

There is not one loyal bone in that bitch's body.

DON: How'd you finally do last night?

TEACH: This has nothing to do with that.

DON: No, I know. I'm just saying . . . for *talk* . .

TEACH: Last night? You were here, Don.

> *Pause.*

How'd *you* do?

DON: Not well.

TEACH: Mmm.

DON: The only one won any money, Fletch and Ruthie.

TEACH *(Pause)*: Cunt had to win two hundred dollars.

DON: She's a good card player.

TEACH: She is *not* a good card player, Don. She is a mooch and she is a locksmith and she plays like a woman.

> *Pause.*

Fletcher's a card player, I'll give him that. But *Ruthie* . . . I
mean, *you see* how she fucking plays . . .

DON: Yeah.

TEACH: And always with that cunt on her shoulder.

DON: Grace?

TEACH: Yes.

DON: Grace is her partner.

TEACH: Then let her *be* her partner, then. (You see what I'm
talking about?) Everyone, they're sitting at the table and
then Grace is going to walk around . . . fetch an *ashtray* . . .
go for *coffee* . . . *this* . . . and everybody's all they aren't
going to hide their cards, and they're going to make a show
how they don't hunch *over,* and like that. I don't give a shit.
I say the broad's her fucking partner, and she walks in back
of me I'm going to hide my hand.

DON: Yeah.

TEACH: And I say anybody doesn't's out of their mind.

Pause.

We're talking about money for chrissake, huh? We're talking about cards. Friendship is friendship, and a wonderful
thing, and I am all for it. I have never said different, and you
know me on this point.

Okay.

But let's just keep it *separate* huh, let's just keep the two
apart, and maybe we can deal with each other like some
human beings.

Pause.

This is all I'm saying, Don. I know you got a soft spot in
your heart for Ruthie . . .

DON: . . . yeah?

TEACH: I know you like the broad and Grace and, Bob, I know
he likes 'em too.

DON: (He likes 'em.)

TEACH: And I like 'em too. (I know, I know.) I m not averse to this. I'm not averse to sitting down. (I know we *will* sit down.) These things happen, I'm not saying that they don't . . . and yeah, yeah, yeah, I know I lost a bundle at the game and blah blah blah.

Pause.

But all I ever ask (and I would say this to her face) is only she remembers who is who and not to go around with *her* or Gracie either with this attitude. "The Past is Past, and this is Now, and so Fuck You."

You see?

DON: Yes.

Long pause.

TEACH: So what's new?

DON: Nothing.

TEACH: Same old shit, huh?

DON: Yup.

TEACH: You seen my hat?

DON: No. Did you leave it here?

TEACH: Yeah.

Pause.

DON: You ask them over at The Riv?

TEACH: I left it here.

Pause.

DON: Well, you left it here, it's here.

TEACH: You seen it?

DON: No.

Pause.

TEACH: Fletch been in?

DON: No.

TEACH: Prolly drop in one or so, huh?

DON: Yeah, You know. You never know with Fletcher.

TEACH: No.

DON: He might drop in the *morning* . . .

TEACH: Yeah.

DON: And then he might, he's gone for ten or fifteen days you never know he's gone.

TEACH: Yeah.

DON: Why?

TEACH: I want to talk to him.

DON *(Pause)*: Ruth would know.

TEACH: You sure you didn't seen my hat?

DON: I didn't see it. No.

    Pause.

Ruthie might know.

TEACH: (Vicious dyke.)

DON: Look in the john.

TEACH: It isn't in the john. I wouldn't leave it there.

DON: Do you got something up with Fletch?

TEACH: No. Just I have to talk to him.

DON: He'll probably show up.

TEACH: Oh yeah . . . *(Pause. Indicating objects on the counter)* What're *these*?

DON: Those?

TEACH: Yeah.

DON: They're from 1933.

TEACH: From the thing?

DON: Yeah.

Pause.

TEACH: Nice.

DON: They had a whole market in 'em. Just like anything. They license out the shit and everybody makes it.

TEACH: Yeah? (I knew that.)

DON: Just like now. They had *combs,* and *brushes* . . . you know, brushes with the thing on 'em . . .

TEACH: Yeah. I know. They had . . . uh . . . what? Clothing too, huh?

DON: I think. Sure. Everything. And there're guys they just collect the stuff.

TEACH: They got that much of it around?

DON: *Shit* yes. (It's not that long ago.) The thing, it ran two years, and they had (*I* don't know) all kinds of people every year they're buying everything that they can lay their hands on that they're going to take it back to Buffalo to give it, you know, to their aunt, and it mounts up.

TEACH: What does it go for?

DON: The compact?

TEACH: Yeah.

DON: Aah . . . (*You* want it?)

TEACH: No.

DON: Oh. I'm just asking. I mean, *you* want it . . .

TEACH: No. I mean somebody walks *in* here . . .

DON: Oh. Somebody walks *in* here . . . (This shit's fashionable . . .)

TEACH: (I don't doubt it.)

DON: . . . and they're gonna have to go like fifteen bucks.

TEACH: You're fulla shit.

DON: My word of honor.

TEACH: No shit.

DON: Everything like that.

TEACH: (A bunch of fucking thieves.)

DON: Yeah. Everything.

TEACH *(snorts)*: What a bunch of crap, huh?

DON: *Oh* yeah.

TEACH: Every goddamn thing.

DON: Yes.

TEACH: If I kept the stuff that I threw *out* . . .

DON: . . . yes.

TEACH: I would be a wealthy man today. I would be cruising on some European yacht.

DON: Uh-huh.

TEACH: (Shit my father used to keep in his *desk* drawer.)

DON: (My father, too.)

TEACH: (The *basement* . . .)

DON: (Uh-huh.)

TEACH: (Fuckin' toys in the backyard, for chrissake . . .)

DON: (Don't even talk about it.)

TEACH: It's . . . I don't know.

>   *Pause.*

You want to play some gin?

DON: Maybe later.

TEACH: Okay.

>   *Pause.*

I dunno.

>   *Pause.*

Fucking *day* . . .

>   *Pause.*

Fucking *weather* . . .

Pause.

DON: You think it's going to rain?

TEACH: Yeah. I do. Later.

DON: Yeah?

TEACH: Well, *look* at it.

>BOB *appears, carrying a paper bag with coffee and foodstuffs in it.*

Bobby, Bobby, Bobby, Bobby, Bobby.

BOB: Ruthie isn't mad at you.

TEACH: She isn't?

BOB: No.

TEACH: How do you know?

BOB: I found out.

TEACH: How?

BOB: I talked to her.

TEACH: You talked to her.

BOB: Yes.

TEACH: I asked you you weren't going to.

BOB: Well, she asked me.

TEACH: What?

BOB: That were you over here.

TEACH: What did you tell her?

BOB: You were here.

TEACH: Oh. *(He looks at* DON.*)*

DON: What did you say to her, Bob?

BOB: Just Teach was here.

DON: And is she coming over here?

BOB: I don't think so. (They had the plain.)

DON *(to* TEACH*)*: So? (This is all right.)
(*To* BOB*)* All right, Bob.

    He looks at TEACH.

TEACH: That's all right, Bob. (*To self*) (Everything's all right to someone . . .)

    DON *takes bag and distributes contents to appropriate recipients.*

(*To* DON*)* You shouldn't eat that shit.

DON: Why?

TEACH: It's just I have a feeling about health foods.

DON: It's not health foods, Teach. It's only yogurt.

TEACH: That's not health foods?

DON: No. They've had it forever.

TEACH: Yogurt?

DON: Yeah. They used to joke about it on "My Little Margie." (*To* BOB*)* (Way before your time.)

TEACH: Yeah?

DON: Yeah.

TEACH: What the fuck. A little bit can't hurt you.

DON: It's *good* for you.

TEACH: Okay, okay. Each one his own opinion. *(Pause. To* BOB*)* Was Fletcher over there?

BOB: No.

DON: Where's my coffee?

BOB: It's not there?

DON: No.

    Pause.

BOB: I told 'em specially to put it in.

DON: Where *is* it?

BOB: They forgot it.

>*Pause.*

>I'll go back and get it.

DON: Would you mind?

BOB: No.

>*Pause.*

DON: You gonna get it?

BOB: Yeah.

>*Pause.*

DON: What, Bob?

BOB: Can I talk to you?

>*Pause.* DON *goes to* BOB.

DON: What is it?

BOB: I saw him.

DON: Who?

BOB: The guy.

DON: You saw the guy?

BOB: Yes.

DON: That I'm talking about?

BOB: Yes.

DON: Just now?

BOB: Yeah. He's going somewhere.

DON: He is.

BOB: Yeah. He's puttin' a suitcase in the car.

DON: The guy, or both of 'em?

BOB: Just him.

DON: He got in the car he drove off??

BOB: He's coming down the stairs . . .

DON: Yeah.

BOB: And he's got the suitcase . . .

    DON *nods.*

He gets in the car . . .

DON: Uh-huh . . .

BOB: He drives away.

DON: So where is she?

BOB: He's goin' to pick her up.

DON: What was he wearing?

BOB: Stuff. Traveling clothes.

DON: Okay.

    Pause.

Now you're talking. You see what I mean?

BOB: Yeah.

DON: All right.

BOB: And he had a coat, too.

DON: Now you're talking.

BOB: Like a raincoat.

DON: Yeah.

    Pause.

Good.

    Pause.

BOB: Yeah, he's gone.

DON: Bob, go get me that coffee, do you mind?

BOB: No.

DON: What did you get yourself to eat?

BOB: I didn't get anything.

DON: Well, get me my coffee, and get yourself something to eat, okay?

BOB: Okay. (Good.) *(Exits.)*

Pause.

DON: How's your bacon?

TEACH: Aaaahh, they always fuck it up.

DON: Yeah.

TEACH: This time they fucked it up too burnt.

DON: Mmmm.

TEACH: You got to be breathing on their neck.

DON: Mmmm.

TEACH: Like a lot of things.

DON: Uh-huh.

TEACH: *Any* business . . .

DON: Yeah.

TEACH: You want it run right, *be* there.

DON: Yeah.

TEACH: Just like you.

DON: What?

TEACH: Like the shop.

DON: Well, no one's going to run it, I'm not here.

Pause.

TEACH: No.

Pause.

You have to be here.

DON: Yeah.

TEACH: It's a one-man show.

DON: Uh-huh.

Pause.

TEACH: So what is this thing with the kid?

Pause.

I mean, is it anything, uh . . .

DON: It's nothing . . . *you* know . .

TEACH: Yeah.

Pause.

It's *what* . . . ?

DON: You know, it's just some *guy* we spotted.

TEACH: Yeah. Some *guy.*

DON: Yeah.

TEACH: (Some guy . . .)

DON: Yeah.

Pause.

What time is it?

TEACH: Noon.

DON: (Noon.) (Fuck.)

TEACH: What?

Pause.

DON: You parked outside?

TEACH: Yeah.

DON: Are you okay on the meter?

TEACH: Yeah. The broad came by already.

Pause.

DON: Good.

Pause.

TEACH: Oh, yeah, she came by.

DON: Good.

TEACH: You want to tell me what this thing is?

DON *(Pause)*: The thing?

TEACH: Yeah.

Pause.

What is it?

DON: Nothing.

TEACH: No? What is it, jewelry?

DON: No. It's nothing.

TEACH: Oh.

DON: You know?

TEACH: Yeah.

Pause.

Yeah. No. I don't know.

Pause.

Who am I, a *police*man . . . I'm making conversation, huh?

DON: Yeah.

TEACH: Huh?

Pause.

'Cause you know I'm just asking for talk.

DON: Yeah. I know. Yeah, okay.

TEACH: And I can live without this.

DON *(reaches for phone)*: Yeah. I know. Hold on, I'll tell you.

TEACH: Tell me if you *want* to, Don.

DON: I want to, Teach.

TEACH: Yeah?
DON: Yeah.

Pause.

TEACH: Well, I'd fucking *hope* so. Am I wrong?

DON: No. No. You're right.

TEACH: I *hope* so.

DON: No, hold on; I gotta make this call.

TEACH: Well, all right. So what is it, jewelry?

DON: No.

TEACH: What?

DON: Coins.

TEACH: (Coins.)

DON: Yeah. Hold on, I gotta make this call.

> DON *hunts for a card, dials telephone.*

(Into phone) Hello? This is Donny Dubrow. We were talking the other day. Lookit, sir, if I could get ahold of some of that stuff you were interested in, would you be interested in some of it?

> *Pause.*

Those *things* . . . *Old,* yeah.

> *Pause.*

Various pieces of various types.

> *Pause.*

Tonight. Sometime late. Are they *what* . . . ! ! ? ? Yes, but I don't see what kind of a question is that (at the prices we're talking about . . .)

> *Pause.*

No, hey, no, I understand *you* . . .

> *Pause.*

Sometime late.

> *Pause.*

One hundred percent.

> *Pause.*

I feel the same. All right. Good-bye. *(Hangs up.)* Fucking asshole.

TEACH: Guys like that, I like to fuck their wives.

DON: I don't blame you.

TEACH: Fucking *jerk* . . .

DON: (I swear to God . . .)

TEACH: That guy's a collector?

DON: Who?

TEACH: The phone guy.

DON: Yeah.

TEACH: And the other guy?

DON: We spotted?

TEACH: Yeah.

DON: Him, too.

TEACH: So you hit him for his coins.

DON: Yeah.

TEACH: —And you got a buyer in the phone guy.

DON: (Asshole.)

TEACH: The thing is you're not sitting with the shit.

DON: No.

TEACH: The guy's an asshole or he's not, what do you care? It's business.

    Pause.

DON: You're right.

TEACH: The guy with the suitcase, he's the mark.

DON: Yeah.

TEACH: How'd you find him?

DON: In here.

TEACH: Came in here, huh?

DON: Yeah.

TEACH: (No shit.)

   Pause.

DON: He comes in here one day, like a week ago.

TEACH: For what?

DON: Just browsing. So he's looking in the case, he comes up
   and with this *buffalo-head* nickel . . .

TEACH: Yeah . . .

DON: From nine*teen*-something. (I don't know. I didn't even
   know it's there . . .)

TEACH: Uh-huh . . .

DON: . . . and he goes, "How much would that be?"

TEACH: Uh-huh . . .

DON: So I'm about to go, "Two bits," jerk that I am, but something tells me to shut up, so I go, "You tell me."

TEACH: Always good business.

DON: *Oh* yeah.

TEACH: How wrong can you go?

DON: That's what I mean, so then he thinks a minute, and he
   tells me he'll just *shop* a bit.

TEACH: Uh-huh . . . (*Stares out of window.*)

DON: And so he's *shopping* . . . What?

TEACH: Some cops.

DON: Where?

TEACH: At the corner.

DON: What are they doing?

TEACH: Cruising.

   Pause.

DON: They turn the corner?

TEACH *(waits)*: *Yeah.*

    Pause.

DON: . . . And so he's shopping. And he's picking up a beat-up *mirror* . . . an old *kid's* toy . . . a *shaving* mug . . .

TEACH: . . . right . . .

DON: Maybe five, six things, comes to eight bucks. I get 'em and I put 'em in a box and then he tells me he'll go fifty dollars for the nickel.

TEACH: No.

DON: Yeah. So I tell him (get this), "Not a chance."

TEACH: (Took balls.)

DON: (Well, what-the-fuck . . .)

TEACH: (No, I mean it.)

DON: (I took a chance.)

TEACH: (You're goddamn right.)

    Pause.

DON *(shrugs)*: So I say, "Not a chance," he tells me eighty is his highest offer.

TEACH: (I knew it.)

DON: Wait. So I go, "Ninety-five."

TEACH: Uh-huh.

DON: We settle down on ninety, *takes* the nickel, leaves the box of shit.

TEACH: He pay for it?

DON: The box of shit?

TEACH: Yeah.

DON: No.

    Pause.

TEACH: And so what was the nickel?

DON: *I* don't know . . . some rarity.

TEACH: Ninety dollars for a nickel.

DON: Are you kidding, Teach? I bet it's worth five *times* that.

TEACH: Yeah, huh?

DON: Are you kidding me, the guy is going to come in here, he plunks down ninety bucks like nothing. *Shit* yeah.

    Pause.

TEACH: Well, what the fuck, it didn't cost you anything.

DON: That's not the point. The next day back he comes and he goes through the whole bit again. He looks at *this*, he looks at *that*, it's a nice *day* . . .

TEACH: Yeah . . .

DON: And he tells me he's the guy was in here yesterday and bought the buffalo off me and do I maybe have some other articles of interest.

TEACH: Yeah.

DON: And so I tell him, "Not offhand." He says that could I get in touch with him, I get some in, so I say "sure," he leaves his card, I'm s'posed to call him anything crops up.

TEACH: Uh-huh.

DON: He comes in here like I'm his fucking doorman.

TEACH: Mmmm.

DON: He takes me off my coin and will I call him if I find another one.

TEACH: Yeah.

DON: Doing me this favor by just coming in my shop.

TEACH: Yeah.

    Pause.

Some people never change.

DON: Like he has done me this big favor by just coming in my shop.

TEACH: Uh-huh. (You're going to get him now.)

DON: (You know I am.) So Bob, we kept a lookout on his place, and that's the shot.

TEACH: And who's the chick?

DON: What chick?

TEACH: You're asking Bob about.

DON: Oh yeah. The guy, he's married. I mean (*I* don't know.) We *think* he's married. They got two names on the bell. . . . Anyway, he's living with this chick, *you* know . . .

TEACH: What the hell.

DON: . . . and you should see this chick.

TEACH: Yeah, huh?

DON: She is a knockout. I mean, she is *real* nice-lookin', Teach.

TEACH: (Fuck *him* . . .)

DON: The other day, last Friday like a week ago, Bob runs in, lugs me out to look at 'em, they're going out on bicycles. The ass on this broad, un-be-fucking-lievable in these bicycling shorts sticking up in the air with these short handlebars.

TEACH: (Fuckin' *fruits* . . .)

> *Pause.*

DON: So that's it. We keep an eye on 'em. They both work. . . . (Yesterday he rode his bicycle to work.)

TEACH: He didn't.

DON: Yeah.

TEACH (*snorts*): (With the three-piece suit, huh?)

DON: I didn't see 'em. Bobby saw 'em.

> *Pause.*

And that's the shot. Earl gets me in touch the phone guy, he's this coin collector, and that's it.

TEACH: It fell in your lap.

DON: Yeah.

TEACH: You're going in tonight.

DON: It looks that way.

TEACH: And who's going in?

    Pause.

DON: Bobby.

    Pause.

He's a good kid, Teach.

TEACH: He's a great kid, Don. You know how I feel about the kid.

    Pause.

I *like* him.

DON: He's doing good.

TEACH: I can see that.

    Pause.

But I gotta say something here.

DON: What?

TEACH: Only this—and I don't think I'm *getting* at anything—

DON: What?

TEACH *(Pause)*: Don't send the kid in.

DON: I shouldn't send Bobby in?

TEACH: No. (Now, just wait a second.) Let's siddown on this. What are we saying here? Loyalty.

    Pause.

You know how I am on this. This is great. This is admirable.

DON: What?

TEACH: This loyalty. This is swell. It turns my heart the things that you do for the kid.

DON: What do I do for him, Walt?

TEACH: Things. Things, you know what I mean.

DON: No. I don't do anything for him.

TEACH: In your mind you don't, but the things, I'm saying, that you actually go *do* for him. This is fantastic. All I mean, a guy can be too loyal, Don. Don't be dense on this. What are we saying here? Business.

I mean, the guy's got you're taking his high-speed blender and a Magnavox, you send the kid in. You're talking about a real *job* . . . they don't come in right away and know they been *had* . . .

You're talking maybe a safe, certainly a good lock or two, and you need a guy's looking for valuable shit, he's not going to mess with the stainless steel silverware, huh, or some digital clock.

   Pause.

We both know what we're saying here. We both know we're talking about some job needs more than the kid's gonna skin-pop go in there with a *crowbar* . . .

DON: I don't want you mentioning that.

TEACH: It slipped out.

DON: You know how I *feel* on that.

TEACH: Yes. And I'm sorry, Don. I admire that. All that I'm saying, don't confuse business with pleasure.

DON: But I don't want that talk, only, Teach.

   Pause.

You understand?

TEACH: I more than understand, and I apologize.

   Pause.

I'm sorry.

DON: That's the only thing.

TEACH: All right. But I tell you. I'm glad I said it.

DON: Why?

TEACH: 'Cause it's best for these things to be out in the open.

DON: But I don't want it in the open.

TEACH: Which is why I apologized.

>   *Pause.*

DON: You know the fucking kid's clean. He's trying hard, he's working hard, and you leave him alone.

TEACH: Oh yeah, he's trying *real* hard

DON: And he's no dummy, Teach.

TEACH: Far from it. All I'm saying, the job is beyond him. Where's the shame in this? This is not jacks, we get up to go home we give everything back. Huh? You want this fucked up?

>   *Pause.*

All that I'm saying, there's the least *chance* something might fuck up, you'd get the law down, you would take the shot, and couldn't find the coins *whatever:* if you see the least chance, you cannot afford to take that chance! Don? *I* want to go in there and gut this motherfucker. Don? Where is the shame in this? You take care of him, *fine.* (Now this is loyalty.) But Bobby's got his own best interests, too. And you cannot afford (and simply as a *business* proposition) you cannot afford to take the chance.

(Pause. TEACH *picks up a strange object.)* What is this?

DON: That?

TEACH: Yes.

DON: It's a thing that they stick in dead pigs keep their legs apart all the blood runs out.

>   TEACH *nods. Pause.*

TEACH: Mmmm.

Pause.

DON: I set it up with him.

TEACH: "You set it up with him." . . . You set it up and then you told him.

Long pause.

DON: I gave Earl ten percent.

TEACH: Yeah? for what?

DON: The connection.

TEACH: So ten off the top: forty-five, forty-five.

Pause.

DON: And Bobby?

TEACH: A hundred. A hundred fifty . . . we hit big . . . *whatever.*

DON: And *you* what? -

TEACH: The *shot.* I *go,* I go *in* . . . I bring the stuff *back* (or wherever . . .)

Pause.

DON: And what do I do?

TEACH: You mind the fort.

Pause.

DON: Here?

TEACH: Well, yeah . . . this is the fort.

Pause.

DON: (You know, this is real classical money we're talking about.)

TEACH: I know it. You think I'm going to fuck with Chump Change?

Pause.

So tell me.

DON: Well, hold on a second. I mean, we're still talking.

TEACH: I'm sorry. I thought we were done talking.

DON: No.

TEACH: Well, then, let's talk some more. You want to bargain? You want to mess with the points?

DON: No. I just want to think for a second.

TEACH: Well, you think, but here's a helpful hint. Fifty percent of some money is better than ninety percent of some broken *toaster* that you're gonna have, you send the kid in. (Which is providing he don't trip the alarm in the *first* place . . .) Don? You don't even know what the *thing* is on this. Where he lives. They got alarms? What *kind* of alarms? What kind of *this* . . . ? And what if (God forbid) the *guy* walks in? Somebody's nervous, whacks him with a table lamp—you wanna get touchy—and you can take your ninety dollars from the nickel shove it up your ass— the good it did you—and you wanna know *why*? (And I'm not *saying* anything . . .) because you didn't take the time to go first-class.

> BOB *re-enters with a bag.*

Hi, Bob.

BOB: Hi, Teach.

> *Pause.*

DON: You get yourself something to eat?

BOB: I got a piece of pie and a Pepsi.

> BOB *and* DON *extract foodstuffs and eat.*

DON: Did they charge you again for the coffee?

BOB: For your coffee?

DON: Yes.

BOB: They charged me this time. I don't know if they charged me last time, Donny.

DON: It's okay.

> *Pause.*

TEACH *(to* BOB*):* How is it out there?

BOB: It's okay.

TEACH: Is it going to rain?

BOB: Today?

TEACH: Yeah.

BOB: I don't know.

>   *Pause.*

TEACH: Well, what do you think?

BOB: It might.

TEACH: You think so, huh?

DON: Teach . . .

TEACH: What? I'm not saying anything.

BOB: What?

TEACH: I don't think I'm saying anything here.

>   *Pause.*

BOB: It *might* rain.

>   *Pause.*

> I think *later.*

TEACH: How's your pie?

BOB: Real good.

TEACH *(holds up the dead-pig leg-spreader):* You know what this is?

>   *Pause.*

BOB: Yeah.

TEACH: What is it?

BOB: I know what it is.

TEACH: What?

BOB: I know.

Pause.

TEACH: Huh?

BOB: What?

TEACH: Things are what they are.

DON: Teach . . .

TEACH: What?

DON: We'll do this later.

BOB: I got to ask you something.

TEACH: Sure, that makes a difference.

DON: We'll just do it later.

TEACH: Sure.

BOB: Uh, Don?

DON: What?

Pause.

BOB: I got to talk to you.

DON: Yeah? What?

BOB: I'm wondering on the thing that maybe I could have a little bit up front.

Pause.

DON: Do you *need* it?

BOB: I don't *need* it . . .

DON: How much?

BOB: I was thinking that maybe you might let me have like fifty or something.

Pause.

To sort of *have* . . .

TEACH: You got any cuff links?

DON: Look in the case. *(To* BOB*)* What do you need it for?

BOB: Nothing.

DON: Bob . . .

BOB: You can trust me.

DON: It's not a question of that. It's not a question I go around
trusting you, Bob . . .

BOB: What's the question?

TEACH: Procedure.

DON: Hold on, Teach.

BOB: I got him all spotted.

Pause.

TEACH: Who?

BOB: Some guy.

TEACH: Yeah?

BOB: Yeah.

TEACH: Where's he live?

BOB: Around.

TEACH: Where? Near here?

BOB: No.

TEACH: No?

BOB: He lives like on Lake Shore Drive.

TEACH: He does.

BOB: Yeah.

TEACH *(Pause)*: What have you got, a job cased?

BOB: I just went for coffee.

TEACH: But you didn't *get* the coffee.

Pause.

Now, did you?

BOB: No.

TEACH: Why?

DON: Hold on, Teach. Bob . . .

BOB: What?

DON: You know what?

BOB: No.

DON: I was thinking, you know, we might hold off on this thing.

Pause.

BOB: You wanna hold *off* on it?

DON: I was thinking that we might.

BOB: Oh.

DON: And, on the money, I'll give you . . . forty, you owe me twenty, and, for now, keep twenty for spotting the guy.

Pause.

Okay?

BOB: Yeah.

Pause.

You don't want me to do the job?

DON: That's what I *told* you. What am I telling you?

BOB: I'm not going to do it.

DON: Not *now*. We aren't going to do it now.

BOB: We'll do it later on?

DON *(shrugs)*: But I'm giving you twenty just for spotting the guy.

BOB: I need fifty, Donny.

DON: Well, I'm giving you forty.

BOB: You said you were giving me twenty.

DON: No, Bob, I did not. I said I was giving you forty, of *which* you were going to owe me twenty.

Pause.

And you go *keep* twenty.

BOB: I got to give back twenty.

DON: That's the deal.

BOB: When?

DON: Soon. When you got it.

    Pause.

BOB: If I don't *get* it soon?

DON: Well, what do you call "soon"?

BOB: I don't know.

DON: Could you get it in a . . . day, or a couple of days or so?

BOB: Maybe. I don't *think* so. Could you let me have fifty?

DON: And you'll give me back thirty?

BOB: I could just give back the twenty.

DON: That's not the deal.

BOB: We could *make* it the deal.

    Pause.

Donny? We could *make* it the deal. Huh?

DON: Bob, lookit. Here it is: I give you fifty, next week you pay me back twenty-five.

    Pause.

You get to keep twenty-five, you pay me back twenty-five.

BOB: And what about the thing?

DON: Forget about it.

BOB: You tell me when you want me to do it.

DON: I don't know *that* I want you to do it. At this point.

    Pause.

You know what I mean?

    Pause.

BOB: No.

DON: I mean, I'm *giving* you twenty-five, and I'm saying forget the thing.

BOB: Forget it for me.

DON: Yes.

BOB: Oh.

   Pause.

   Okay. Okay.

DON: You see what I'm talking about?

BOB: Yes.

DON: Like it never happened.

BOB: I know.

DON: So you see what I'm saying.

BOB: Yes.

   Pause.

   I'm gonna go.

   Pause.

   I'll see you later. *(Pause. He looks at DON.)*

DON: Oh. *(Reaches in pocket and hands bills to BOB. To TEACH)* You got two fives?

TEACH: No.

DON *(to BOB)*: I got to give you . . . thirty, you owe me back thirty.

BOB: You said you were giving me fifty.

DON: I'm sorry, I'm sorry, Bob, you're absolutely right. *(He gives BOB remainder of money.)*

   Pause.

BOB: Thank you.

   Pause.

I'll see you later, huh, Teach?

TEACH: I'll see you later, Bobby.

BOB: I'll see you, Donny.

DON: I'll see you later, Bob.

BOB: I'll come back later.

DON: Okay.

> BOB *starts to exit.*

TEACH: *See* you.

> *Pause.* BOB *is gone.*

You're only doing the right thing by him, Don.

> *Pause.*

Believe me.

> *Pause.*

It's best for everybody.

> *Pause.*

What's done is done.

> *Pause.*

So let's get started. On the thing. Tell me everything.

DON: Like what?

TEACH: . . . the *guy* . . . where does he *live* . . .

DON: Around the corner.

TEACH: Okay, and he's gone for the weekend.

DON: We don't know.

TEACH: Of course we know. Bob saw him coming out the door. The kid's not going to lie to you.

DON: Well, Bob just saw him coming *out* . . .

TEACH: He had a suitcase, Don, he wasn't going to the A&P . . . He's going for the weekend . . .

Pause.

Don, (Can you cooperate?) Can we get started? Do you want to tell me something about coins?

Pause.

DON: What about 'em?

TEACH: A crash course. What to look for. What to take. What to *not* take (. . . this they can trace) (that isn't *worth* nothing . . .)

Pause.

What looks like what but it's more *valuable . . . so* on . . .

DON: First off, I want that nickel back.

TEACH: Donny . . .

DON: No, I know, it's only a fuckin' nickel . . . I mean big deal, huh? But what I'm saying is I only want it back.

TEACH: You're going to get it back. I'm going in there for his coins, what am I going to take 'em all except your nickel? Wake up. Don, let's plan this out. The *spirit* of the thing?

Pause.

Let's not be loose on this. People are *loose,* people pay the price . . .

DON: You're right.

TEACH: (And I like you like a brother, Don.) So let's wake up on this.

Pause.

All right? A man, he walks in here, well-dressed . . . (With a briefcase?)

DON: (No.)

TEACH: All right. . . . comes into a junkshop looking for coins.

Pause.

He spots a valuable nickel hidden in a pile of shit. He farts around, he picks up this, he farts around, he picks up that.

DON: (He wants the nickel.)

TEACH: No shit. He goes to check out, he goes ninety on the nick.

DON: (He would of gone five times that.)

TEACH: (Look, don't kick yourself.) All right, we got a guy knows coins. Where does he keep his coin collection?

DON: Hidden.

TEACH: The man hides his coin collection, we're probably looking the guy has a *study* . . . I mean, he's not the kind of guy to keep it in the *basement* . . .

DON: No.

TEACH: So we're looking for a study.

DON: (A den.)

TEACH: And we're looking, for, he hasn't got a *safe* . . .

DON: Yeah . . . ?

TEACH: . . . he's probably going to keep 'em . . . where?

    Pause.

DON: I don't know. His desk drawer.

TEACH: (You open the middle, the rest of 'em pop out?)

DON: (Yeah.)

TEACH: (Maybe.) Which brings up a point.

DON: What?

TEACH: As we're moving the stuff tonight, we can go in like Gangbusters, huh? We don't care we wreck the joint up. So what else? We *take* it, or leave it?

DON: . . . well . . .

TEACH: I'm not talking *cash*, all I mean, what other stuff do we take . . . for our *trouble* . . .

    Pause.

DON: I don't know.

TEACH: It's hard to make up rules about this stuff.

DON: (You'll be in there under lots of pressure.)

TEACH: (Not so much.)

DON: (Come on, a little, anyway.)

TEACH: (That's only natural.)

DON: (Yeah.)

TEACH: (It would be unnatural I wasn't tense. A guy who isn't tense, I don't want him on my side.)

DON: (No.)

TEACH: (You know *why*?)

DON: (Yeah.)

TEACH: (Okay, then.) It's good to talk this stuff out.

DON: Yeah.

TEACH: You *have* to talk it out. Bad feelings, misunderstandings happen on a job. You can't get away from 'em, you have to deal with 'em. You want to quiz me on some coins? You want to show some coins to me? *List* prices . . . the blue book . . . ?

DON: You want to see the book?

TEACH: Sure.

DON *(hands large coin-book to* TEACH*)*: I just picked it up last week.

TEACH: Uh-hum.

DON: All the values aren't *current* . . .

TEACH: Uh-huh . . .

DON: *Silver* . . .

TEACH *(looking at book)*: Uh-huh . . .

DON: What's *rarity* . . .

TEACH: Well, that's got to be fairly steady, huh?

DON: I'm saying against what *isn't*.

TEACH: Oh.

DON: But the book gives you a general idea.

TEACH: You've been looking at it?

DON: Yeah.

TEACH: You got to have a feeling for your subject.

DON: The book can give you that.

TEACH: This is what I'm *saying* to you. One thing. Makes all the
difference in the world.

DON: What?

TEACH: Knowing what the fuck you're talking about. And it's so
rare, Don. *So* rare.

What do you think a 1929 S Lincoln-head penny with the
wheat on the back is worth?

DON *starts to speak.*

Ah! Ah! Ah! Ah! Ah! We got to know what *condition* we're
talking about.

DON *(Pause)*: Okay. What condition?

TEACH: *Any* of 'em. You tell me.

DON: Well, pick one.

TEACH: Okay, I'm going to pick an easy one. Excellent condition 1929 S.

DON: It's worth . . . *about* thirty-six dollars.

TEACH: No.

DON: (More?)

TEACH: Well, guess.

DON: Just tell me is it more or less.

TEACH: What do you think?

DON: More.

TEACH: No.

DON: Okay, it's worth, I gotta say . . . eighteen-sixty.

TEACH: No.

DON: Then I give up.

TEACH: Twenty fucking cents.

DON: You're fulla shit.

TEACH: My mother's grave.

DON: Give me that fucking book. *(Business.)* Go beat that.

TEACH: This is what I'm saying, Don, you got to know what you're talking about.

DON: You wanna take the book?

TEACH: Naaa, *fuck* the book. What am I going to do, leaf through the book for hours on end? The important thing is to have the *idea* . . .

DON: Yeah.

TEACH: What was the other one?

DON: What other one?

TEACH: He stole off you.

DON: What do you mean what was it?

TEACH: The *date*, so on.

DON: How the fuck do *I* know?

TEACH *(Pause)*: When you looked it up.

DON: How are you getting in the house?

TEACH: The house?

DON: Yeah.

TEACH: Aah, you go in through a *window* they left open, something.

DON: Yeah.

TEACH: There's always something.

DON: Yeah. What else, if not the window.

TEACH: How the fuck do *I* know?

>   *Pause.*

> If not the window, something else.

DON: What?

TEACH: We'll see when we get there.

DON: Okay, all I'm asking, what it *might* be.

TEACH: Hey, you didn't warn us we were going to have a *quiz* . . .

DON: It's just a question.

TEACH: I know it.

>   *Pause.*

DON: What is the answer?

TEACH: We're seeing when we get there.

DON: Oh. You can't answer me, Teach?

TEACH: You have your job, I have my job, Don. I am not here to smother you in theory. Think about it.

DON: I am thinking about it. I'd like you to answer my question.

TEACH: Don't push me, Don. Don't front off with me here. I am not other people.

DON: And just what does that mean?

TEACH: Just that nobody's perfect.

DON: They aren't.

TEACH: No.

>   *Pause.*

DON: I'm going to have Fletch come with us.

TEACH: Fletch.

DON: Yes.

TEACH: You're having him *come* with us.

DON: Yes.

TEACH: Now you're kidding me.

DON: No.

TEACH: No? Then why do you say this?

DON: With Fletch.

TEACH: Yes.

DON: I want some depth.

TEACH: You want depth on the team.

DON: Yes, I do.

TEACH: So you bring in Fletch.

DON: Yes.

TEACH: 'Cause I don't play your games with you.

DON: We just might need him.

TEACH: We won't.

DON: We might, Teach.

TEACH: We don't need him, Don. We do not need this guy.

> DON *picks up phone.*

What? Are you *calling* him?

> DON *nods.*

DON: It's busy. *(Hangs up.)*

TEACH: He's probably talking on the phone.

DON: Yeah. He probably is.

TEACH: We don't need this guy, Don. We don't need him. I see your point here, I do. So you're thinking I'm out there alone, and you're worried I'll rattle, so you ask me how I go in. I understand. I see this, I do. I could go in the second floor, climb up a drainpipe, I could *this* . . .

> DON *dials phone again.*

He's talking, he's talking, for chrissake, give him a minute, huh?

DON *hangs up phone.*

I am hurt, Don.

DON: I'm sorry, Teach.

TEACH: I'm not hurt for me.

DON: Who are you hurt for?

TEACH: Think about it.

DON: We can use somebody watch our rear.

TEACH: You keep your numbers down, you don't *have* a rear. You know what has rears? Armies.

DON: I'm just saying, something goes *wrong* . . .

TEACH: Wrong, wrong, you make your own right and wrong. Hey Biiig fucking deal. The shot is yours, no one's disputing that. We're talking business, let's *talk* business: you think it's good business call Fletch in? To help us.

DON: Yes.

TEACH: Well then okay.

> *Pause.*

Are you sure?

DON: Yeah.

TEACH: All right, if you're *sure* . . .

DON: I'm sure, Teach.

TEACH: Then, all right, then. That's all I worry about.

> *Pause.*

And you're probably right, we could use three of us on the job.

DON: Yeah.

TEACH: Somebody watch for the *cops* . . . work out a *signal* . . .

DON: Yeah.

TEACH: Safety in numbers.

DON: Yeah.

TEACH: Three-men jobs.

DON: Yeah.

TEACH: You, me, Fletcher.

DON: Yeah.

TEACH: A division of labor.

> *Pause.*

(Security. Muscle. Intelligence.) Huh?

DON: Yeah.

TEACH: This means, what, a traditional split. Am I right? We get ten off the top goes to Earl, and the rest, three-way split. Huh? That's what we got? Huh?

DON: Yeah.

TEACH: Well, that's what's right.

> *Pause.*

All right. Lay the shot out for me.

DON: For tonight?

TEACH: Yes.

DON: Okay.

> *Pause.*

I stay here on the phone . . .

TEACH: . . . yeah . . .

DON: . . . for Fletcher . . .

TEACH: Yeah.

DON: We meet, ten-thirty, 'leven, back here.

TEACH: (Back here, the three . . .)

DON: Yeah. And go in.

Pause.

Huh?

TEACH: Yeah. Where?

DON: Around the corner.

TEACH: Yeah.

Pause.

Are you mad at me?

DON: No.

TEACH: Do you want to play gin?

DON: Naaa.

TEACH: Then I guess I'll go home, take a nap, and rest up. Come back here tonight and we'll take off this fucking fruit's coins.

DON: Right.

TEACH: I feel like I'm trying to stay *up* to death . . .

DON: You ain't been to sleep since the game?

TEACH: *Shit* no (then that dyke cocksucker . . .)

DON: So go take a nap. You trying to kill yourself?

TEACH: You're right, and you do what you think is right, Don.

DON: I got to, Teach.

TEACH: You got to trust your instincts, right or wrong.

DON: I got to.

TEACH: I know it. I know you do.

Pause.

Anybody wants to get in touch with me, I'm over the hotel.

DON: Okay.

TEACH: I'm not the *hotel,* I stepped out for coffee, I'll be back one minute.

DON: Okay.

TEACH: And I'll *see* you around *eleven*.

DON: O'*clock*.

TEACH: *Here*.

DON: Right.

TEACH: And don't worry about anything.

DON: I won't.

TEACH: I don't want to hear you're worrying about a god-damned thing.

DON: You won't, Teach.

TEACH: You're sure you want Fletch coming with us?

DON: Yes.

TEACH: All right, then, so long as you're sure.

DON: I'm sure, Teach.

TEACH: Then I'm going to see you tonight.

DON: Goddamn right you are.

TEACH: I am seeing you later.

DON: I know.

TEACH: Good-bye.

DON: Good-bye.

TEACH: I want to make one thing plain before I go, Don. I am not mad at you.

DON: I know.

TEACH: All right, then.

DON: You have a good nap.

TEACH: I will.

TEACH *exits.*

DON: Fuckin' *business . . .*

Lights dim to black.

ACT II

Don's Resale Shop. 11:15 that evening. The shop is darkened. DON *is alone. He is holding the telephone to his ear.*

DON: Great. Great great great great great.

Pause.

(*Cocksucking* fuckhead . . .)

Pause.

This is greatness.

DON *hangs up phone.* BOB *appears in the door to the shop.*

What are you doing here?

BOB: I *came* here.

DON: For what?

BOB: I got to talk to you.

DON: Why?

BOB: Business.

DON: Yeah?

BOB: I need some money.

DON: What for?

BOB: Nothing. I can pay for it.

DON: For what?

BOB: This guy. I found a coin.

DON: A coin?

BOB: A buffalo-head.

DON: Nickel?

BOB: Yeah. You want it?

Pause.

DON: What are you doing here, Bob?

BOB: I need money.

DON *picks up phone and dials. He lets it ring as he talks to* BOB.

You want it?

DON: What?

BOB: My buffalo.

DON: Lemme look at it.

> *Pause.*

I got to look at it to know do I want it.

BOB: You don't know if you want it?

DON: I probably *want* it . . . what I'm saying, if it's *worth* anything.

BOB: It's a buffalo, it's worth something.

DON: The question is but what. It's just like everything else, Bob. Like every other fucking thing. *(Pause. He hangs up phone.)* Were you at The Riv?

BOB: Before.

DON: Is Fletch over there?

BOB: No.

DON: Teach?

BOB: No. Ruth and Gracie was there for a minute.

DON: What the fuck does that mean?

> *Pause.*

BOB: Nothing.

> *Pause.*

Only they were there.

> *Pause.*

I didn't *mean* anything . . . my nickel . . . I can tell you what it is.

> *Pause.*

I can tell you what it is.

DON: What? What *date* it is? That don't mean shit.

BOB: No?

DON: Come *on*, Bobby? What's important in a coin . . .

BOB: . . . yeah?

DON: What *condition* it's in . . .

BOB: (Great.)

DON: . . . if you can (I don't know . . .) count the hair on the Indian, something. You got to look it up.

BOB: In the book?

DON: Yes.

BOB: Okay. And then you know.

DON: Well, no. What I'm saying, the book is like you use it like an *indicator* (I mean, right off with *silver* prices . . . so on . . .) *(He hangs up phone.)* Shit.

BOB: What?

DON: What do you want for the coin?

BOB: What it's worth only.

DON: Okay, we'll look it up.

BOB: But you still don't know.

DON: But you got an idea, Bob. You got an idea you can *deviate* from.

    Pause.

BOB: The other guy went ninety bucks.

DON: He was a fuckin' sucker, Bob.

    Pause.

Am I a sucker? (Bob, I'm busy here. You *see*?)

BOB: Some coins are worth that.

DON: Oddities, Bob. Freak oddities of nature. What are we

talking about here? The silver? The silver's maybe three times face. You want fifteen cents for it?

BOB: No.

DON: So, okay. So what do you want for it?

BOB: What it's worth.

DON: Let me see it.

BOB: Why?

DON: To look in the goddamn . . . Forget it. Forget it. *Don't* let me see it.

BOB: But the book don't *mean* shit.

DON: The book gives us *ideas,* Bob. The book gives us a basis for *comparison.*

Look, we're human beings. We can *talk,* we can negotiate, we can *this* . . . you need money? What do you need?

Pause.

BOB: I *came* here . . .

Pause.

DON: What do you need, Bob?

Pause.

BOB: How come you're in here so late?

DON: We're gonna play cards.

BOB: Who?

DON: Teach and me and Fletcher.

TEACH *enters the store.*

What time is it?

TEACH: Fuck is *he* doing here?

DON: What fucking time is it?

TEACH: Where's Fletcher?

Pause.

Where's Fletcher?

BOB: Hi, Teach.

TEACH *(to* DON*)*: What is he doing here?

BOB: I came in.

DON: Do you know what time it is?

TEACH: What? I'm late?

DON: Damn right you're late.

TEACH: I'm fucked up since my watch broke.

DON: Your watch broke?

TEACH: I just told you that.

DON: When did your watch break?

TEACH: The fuck do *I* know?

DON: Well, you look at it. You want to know your watch broke, all you got to do is look at it.

 Pause.

TEACH: I don't have it.

DON: Why not?

TEACH: I took it off when it broke. (What do you *want* here?)

DON: You're going around without a watch.

TEACH: Yes. I am, Donny. What am I, you're my *keeper* all a sudden?

DON: I'm paying you to do a thing, Teach, I expect to know where you are when.

TEACH: Donny. You aren't paying me to do a thing. We are doing something together. I know we are. My watch broke, that is my concern. The *thing* is your and my concern. And the concern of Fletcher. You want to find a reason we should jump all over each other all of a sudden like we work in a *bloodbank*, fine. But it's not good business.

 Pause.

And so who knows what time it is offhand? Jerks on the radio? The phone broad?

Pause.

Now, I understand nerves.

DON: There's no fuckin' nerves involved in this. Teach.

TEACH: No, huh?

DON: No.

TEACH: Well, great. That's great, then. So what are we talking about? A little lateness? Some excusable fucking lateness? And a couple of guys they're understandably a bit excited?

Pause.

DON: I don't like it.

TEACH: Then *don't* like it, then. Let's do this. Let's everybody get a writ. I got a case. You got a case. Bobby—I don't know what the fuck *he's* doing here . . .

DON: Leave him alone.

TEACH: Now I'm picking on him.

DON: Leave him alone.

TEACH: What's he doing here?

DON: He came in.

BOB: I found a nickel.

TEACH: Hey, that's fantastic.

BOB: You want to see it?

TEACH: Yes, please let me see it.

BOB *(hands nickel, wrapped in cloth, to* TEACH*):* I like 'em because of the art on it.

TEACH: Uh-huh.

BOB: Because it *looks* like something.

TEACH *(to* DON*):* Is this worth anything?

BOB: We don't know yet.

TEACH: Oh.

BOB: We're going to look it up.

TEACH: Oh, what? Tonight?

BOB: I think so.

DON *(hangs up phone)*: Fuck.

TEACH: So where is he?

DON: How the fuck do I know?

TEACH: He said he'd be here?

DON: Yes, he did, Teach.

BOB: Fletcher?

TEACH: So where is he, then? And what's *he* doing here?

DON: Leave him alone. He'll leave.

TEACH: He's going to leave, huh?

DON: Yes.

TEACH: You're sure it isn't like the bowling league, Fletch doesn't show up, we just suit up Bobby, give him a shot, and *he* goes in?

    Pause.

Aaah, fuck. I'm sorry. I spoke in anger. I'm sorry, I'm sorry. (Everybody can make mistakes around here but me.) I'm sorry, Bob, I'm very sorry.

BOB: That's okay, Teach.

TEACH: All I meant to say, we'd give you a fuckin' suit, like in football . . .

    Pause.

and you'd (You know, like, whatever . . .) and *you'd* go in. *(Pause. To* DON*)* So what do you want me to do? Dress up and lick him all over? I said I was sorry, what's going on here. Huh? In the *first* place. I come in, I'm *late* . . . he's here . . .

    Pause.

DON: Bobby, I'll see you tomorrow, okay? *(He picks phone up and dials.)*

BOB: I need some money.

TEACH *(digging in pockets)*: What do you need?

BOB: I want to sell the *buffalo* nickel.

TEACH: I'll buy it myself.

BOB: We don't know what it's worth.

TEACH: What do you want for it?

BOB: Fifty dollars.

TEACH: You're outta your fuckin' mind.

> *Pause.*

Look. Here's a fin. Get lost. Okay?

> *Pause.*

BOB: It's worth more than that.

TEACH: How the fuck do you know that?

BOB: I think it is.

> *Pause.*

TEACH: Okay. You keep the fin like a loan. You *keep* the fuckin' nickel, and we'll call it a loan. Now go on. *(He hands nickel back to* BOB.*)*

DON *(hangs up phone)*: Fuck.

BOB: I need more.

TEACH *(to* DON*)*: Give the kid a couple of bucks.

DON: What?

TEACH: Give him some money.

DON: What for?

TEACH: The nickel.

> *Pause.*

BOB: We can look in the book tomorrow.

DON *(to* TEACH*)*: You bought the nickel?

TEACH: Don't worry about it. Give him some money. Get him out of here.

DON: How much?

TEACH: What? *I* don't care . . .

DON *(to* BOB*)*: How much . . . *(To* TEACH*)* What the fuck am I giving him money for?

TEACH: Just give it to him.

DON: What? Ten? *(Pause. Digs in pocket, hands bill to* BOB*.)* How is that, Bob? *(Pause. Hands additional bill to* BOB*.)* Okay?

BOB: We'll look it up.

DON: Okay. Huh? We'll see you tomorrow.

BOB: And we'll look it up.

DON: Yes.

BOB *(to* TEACH*)*: You should talk to Ruthie.

TEACH: Oh, I should, huh?

BOB: Yes.

TEACH: Why?

BOB: Because.

> *Pause.*

TEACH: I'll see you tomorrow, Bobby.

BOB: Good-bye, Teach.

TEACH: Good-bye.

DON: Good-bye, Bob.

BOB: Good-bye.

> *Pause.* BOB *exits.*

DON: Fuckin' *kid* . . .

TEACH: So where is Fletcher?

DON: Don't worry. He'll be here.

TEACH: The question is but when. Maybe his watch broke.

DON: Maybe it just did, Teach. Maybe his actual watch broke.

TEACH: And maybe mine didn't, you're saying? You wanna bet? You wanna place a little fucking wager on it? How much money you got in your pockets? I bet you all the money in your pockets against all the money in my pockets, I walk out that door right now, I come back with a broken watch.

   Pause.

DON: Calm down.

TEACH: I am calm. I'm just upset.

DON: I know.

TEACH: So where is he when I'm here?

DON: Don't worry about it.

TEACH: So who's going to worry about it then?

DON: (Shit.)

TEACH: This should go to prove you something.

DON: It doesn't prove anything. The guy's just late.

TEACH: Oh. And I wasn't?

DON: You were late, too.

TEACH: You're fuckin' A I was, and I got bawled out for it.

DON: He's late for a reason.

TEACH: I don't accept it.

DON: That's your privilege.

TEACH: And what was Bob doing here?

DON: He told you. He wanted to sell me the nickel.

TEACH: That's why he came here?

DON: Yes.

TEACH: To sell you the buffalo?

DON: Yes.

TEACH: Where did he get it?

DON: I think from some guy.

TEACH: Who?

>*Pause.*

DON: I don't know.

>*Pause.*

TEACH: Where's Fletcher?

DON: I don't know. He'll show up. *(Picks up phone and dials.)*

TEACH: He'll show up.

DON: Yes.

TEACH: He's not here now.

DON: No.

TEACH: You scout the guy's house?

DON: The guy? No.

TEACH: Well, let's do that, then. (He's not home. Hang up.)

DON *(hangs up phone)*: You wanna scout his house.

TEACH: Yeah.

DON: Why? Bob already saw him when he went off with the suitcase.

TEACH: Just to be sure, huh?

DON: Yeah. Okay.

TEACH: You bet. Now we call him up.

DON: We call the guy up.

TEACH: Yeah.

>*Pause.*

DON: Good idea. *(He picks up phone. Hunts guy's number. Dials. To himself)* We can do this.

TEACH: This is planning. . . . This is preparation. If he answers . . .

> DON *shhhhs* TEACH.

I'm telling you what to do if he answers.

DON: What?

TEACH: Hang up. (DON *starts to hang up phone.*) No. *Don't* hang up. Hang up now. Hang up *now*!

> DON *hangs up phone.*

Now look: If he *answers* . . .

DON: . . . yeah?

TEACH: *Don't* arouse his fucking suspicions.

DON: All right.

TEACH: And the odds are he's not there, so when he answers just say you're calling for a wrong fucking *number*, something. Be simple.

> *Pause.*

Give me the phone.

> DON *hands* TEACH *the phone.*

Gimme the card.

> DON *hands* TEACH *card.*

This is his number? 221—7834?

DON: Yeah.

TEACH *(snorts)*: All right. I dial, I'm calling for somebody named June, and we go interchange on number.

> *Pause.*

We're gonna say like, "Is this 221—7834?"

DON: . . . yeah?

TEACH: And they go, "No." (I mean "—7843." It *is* —7834.)

So we go, very simply, "Is this 221—7843?" and they go "No," and right away the guy is home, we still haven't blown the shot.

DON: Okay.

> TEACH *picks up the phone and dials.*

TEACH *(into phone)*: Hi. Yeah. I'm calling . . . uh . . . is June there?

> *Pause.*

Well, is this 221—7843?

> *Pause.*

It is? Well, look I must of got the number wrong. I'm sorry.

> *He hangs up phone.*

(This is bizarre.) Read me that number.

DON: 221—7834.

TEACH: Right. *(Dials phone. Listens.)* Nobody home. See, this is careful operation . . . *(Pause. Hangs up.) You* wanna try it?

DON: No.

TEACH: I don't mind that you're careful, Don. This doesn't piss me off. What gets me mad, when you get loose.

DON: What do you mean?

TEACH: You know what I mean.

DON: No, I don't.

TEACH: Yes you do. I come in here. The kid's here.

DON: He doesn't know anything.

TEACH: He doesn't.

DON: No.

TEACH: What was he here for, then?

DON: Sell me the buffalo.

TEACH: Sell it tonight.

DON: Yeah.

TEACH: A valuable nickel.

DON: We don't know.

   Pause.

TEACH: Where is Fletch?

DON: I don't know. *(Picks up phone and dials.)*

TEACH: He's not home. He's not home, Don. He's out.

DON *(into phone)*: Hello?

TEACH: He's in?

DON: This is Donny Dubrow.

TEACH: The Riv?

DON: I'm looking for Fletcher.

   Pause.

 Okay. Thank you. *(He hangs up.)*

TEACH: Cocksucker should be horsewhipped with a horsewhip.

DON: He'll show up.

TEACH: Fucking Riverside, too. (Thirty-seven cents for take-out coffee . . .)

DON: Yeah. *(Picks up phone.)*

TEACH: A lot of nerve you come in there for sixteen years. This is not free enterprise.

DON: No.

TEACH: You know what is free enterprise?

DON: No. What?

TEACH: The freedom . . .

DON: . . . yeah?

TEACH: Of the *Individual* . . .

DON: . . . yeah?

TEACH: To Embark on Any Fucking Course that he sees fit.

DON: Uh-huh . . .

TEACH: In order to secure his honest chance to make a profit. Am I so out of line on this?

DON: No.

TEACH: Does this make me a Commie?

DON: No.

TEACH: The country's *founded* on this, Don. You know this.

DON: Did you get a chance to take a nap?

TEACH: Nap nap nap nap nap. Big deal.

DON *(Pause)*: Yeah.

TEACH: Without this we're just savage shitheads in the wilderness.

DON: Yeah.

TEACH: Sitting around some vicious campfire. That's why *Ruthie* burns me up.

DON: Yeah.

TEACH: (Nowhere dyke . . .) And take those fuckers in the concentration camps. You think they went in there by *choice?*

DON: No.

TEACH: They were *dragged* in there, Don . . .

DON: . . . yeah.

TEACH: Kicking and screaming. *Gimme* that fucking phone.

    TEACH *grabs phone. Listens. Hangs up.*

He's not home. I say *fuck* the cocksucker.

DON: He'll show up.

TEACH: You believe that?

DON: Yes.

TEACH: Then you are full of shit.

DON: Don't tell me that, Teach. Don't tell me I'm full of shit.

TEACH: I'm sorry. You want me to hold your hand? This is how you keep score. I mean, *we're* all here . . .

DON: Just, I don't want that talk.

TEACH: Don . . . I talk straight to you 'cause I respect you. It's kickass or kissass, Don, and I'd be lying if I told you any different.

DON: And what makes you such an authority on life all of a sudden?

TEACH: My life, Jim. And the way I've lived it.

> *Pause.*

DON: Now what does that mean, Teach?

TEACH: What does that mean?

DON: Yes.

TEACH: What does that *mean*?

DON: Yes.

TEACH: Nothing. Not a thing. All that I'm telling you, the shot is yours. It's one night only. Too many guys know. All I'm saying. Take your shot.

DON: Who knows?

TEACH: You and me.

DON: Yeah.

TEACH: Bob and Fletcher. Earl, the phone guy, Grace and Ruthie, maybe.

DON: Grace and Ruth don't know.

TEACH: Who *knows* they know or not, all that I'm telling you, it's not always so clear what's going on. Like Fletcher and the pig iron, that time.

DON: What was the shot on that?

TEACH: He stole some pig iron off Ruth.

DON: (I *heard* that . . .)

TEACH: That's a fact. A fact stands by itself. And we must face the facts and act on them. You better wake up, Don, right now, or things are going to fall around your *head,* and you are going to turn around to find he's took the joint off by himself.

DON: He would not do that.

TEACH: He would. He is an animal.

DON: He don't have the address.

TEACH: He doesn't know it.

DON: No.

TEACH: Now, that is wise. Then let us go and take what's ours.

DON: We have a deal with the man.

TEACH: With Fletcher.

DON: Yes.

TEACH: We had a deal with Bobby.

DON: What does that mean?

TEACH: Nothing.

DON: It don't.

TEACH: No.

DON: What did you mean by that?

TEACH: I didn't mean a thing.

DON: You didn't.

TEACH: No.

DON: You're full of shit, Teach.

TEACH: I am.

DON: Yes.

TEACH: Because I got the balls to face some facts?

Pause.

You scare me sometimes, Don.

DON: Oh, yeah?

TEACH: Yes. I don't want to go around with you here, things go down, we'll settle when we're done. We have a job to do here. Huh? Forget it. Let's go, come on.

DON: We're waiting for him.

TEACH: Fletcher.

DON: Yes.

TEACH: Why?

DON: Many reasons.

TEACH: Tell me one. You give me one good reason, why we're sitting here, and I'll sit down and never say a word. One reason. One. Go on. I'm listening.

DON: He knows how to get in.

Pause.

TEACH: Good night, Don. *(He starts to go for door.)*

DON: Where are you going?

TEACH: Home.

DON: You're going home.

TEACH: Yes.

DON: Why?

TEACH: You're fucking with me. It's all right.

DON: Hold on. You tell me how I'm fucking with you.

TEACH: Come *on,* Don.

DON: You asked me the one reason.

TEACH: You make yourself ridiculous.

DON: Yeah?

TEACH: Yeah.

DON: Then answer it.

TEACH: What is the question?

DON: Fletch knows how to get in.

TEACH: "Get in." That's your reason?

DON: Yes.

> *Pause.*

TEACH: What the fuck they live in Fort Knox? ("Get in.") *(Snorts.)* You break in a *window,* worse comes to worse you kick the fucking *back door* in. (What do you think this is, the Middle Ages?)

DON: What about he's got a safe?

TEACH: Biiiig fucking deal.

DON: How is that?

TEACH: You want to know about a safe?

DON: Yes.

TEACH: What you do, a *safe* . . . you find the combination.

DON: Where he wrote it down.

TEACH: Yes.

DON: What if he didn't write it down?

TEACH: He wrote it down. He's *gotta* write it down. What happens he forgets it?

DON: What happens he doesn't forget it?

TEACH: He's gotta forget it, Don. Human nature. The point being, even he *doesn't* forget it, *why* does he not forget it?

DON: Why?

TEACH: 'Cause he's got it *wrote down.*

> *Pause.*

That's why he *writes* it down.

> *Pause.*

Huh? Not because he's some fucking turkey can't even remember the combination to his own *safe* . . . but only in the event that (God forbid) he somehow *forgets* it . . . he's got it wrote down.

Pause.

This is common sense.

Pause.

What's the good keep the stuff in the safe, every time he wants to get at it he's got to write away to the manufacturer?

DON: Where does he write it?

TEACH: What difference? *Here* . . . We go in, I find the combination fifteen minutes, tops.

Pause.

There are only just so many places it could be. Man is a creature of habits. Man does not change his habits overnight. This is not like him. (And if he does, he has a very good reason.) Look, Don: You want to remember something (you write it down). Where do you put it?

Pause.

DON: In my wallet.

Pause.

TEACH: *Exactly!*

Pause.

Okay?

DON: What if he didn't write it down?

TEACH: He wrote it down.

DON: I know he did. But just, I'm saying, from *another* instance. Some made-up guy from my imagination.

TEACH: You're saying in the instance of some guy . . .

DON: (Some *other* guy . . .)

TEACH: . . . he didn't write it down?

Pause.

DON: Yes.

TEACH: Well, this is another thing.

Pause.

You see what I'm saying?

DON: Yeah.

TEACH: It's another matter. The guy, he's got the shit in the safe, he didn't write it *down* . . .

Pause.

Don . . . ?

DON: Yes?

TEACH: How do you know he didn't write it down?

DON: (I'm, you know, making it up.)

Pause.

TEACH: Well, then, this is not based on *fact.*

Pause.

You see what I'm saying?

I can sit here and tell you *this*, I can tell you *that*, I can tell you any fucking thing you care to mention, but what is the point?

You aren't telling me he didn't write it down. All that you're saying, you can't *find* it. Which is only natural, as you don't know where to look. All I'm asking for a little trust here.

DON: I don't know.

TEACH: Then you know what? Fuck you. (All day long. Grace and Ruthie Christ) What am I standing here convincing you? What am I doing demeaning myself standing here pleading with you to protect your best interests? I can't believe this, Don. Somebody told me I'd do this for you . . . (For *anybody*) I'd call him a liar. (I'm coming in here to efface myself.) I am not Fletch, Don, no, and you should thank God and fall *down* I'm not. (You're coming in here all the time that "He's so good at cards . . . ") The man is a cheat, Don. He *cheats* at cards—Fletcher, the guy that you're waiting for.

DON: He cheats.

TEACH: Fucking A right, he does.

DON: Where do you get this?

>   *Pause.*

You're full of shit, Walt. You're saying Fletch cheats at cards.

>   *Pause.*

You've seen him. You've *seen* him he cheats.

>   *Pause.*

You're *telling* me this?

TEACH: (The whatchamacallit is always the last to know.)

DON: Come on, Walt, I mean, forget with the job and all.

TEACH: You live in a world of your own, Don.

DON: Fletch cheats at cards.

TEACH: Yes.

DON: I don't believe you.

TEACH: Ah. You can't take the truth.

DON: No. I am sorry. I play in this fucking game.

TEACH: And you don't know what goes on.

DON: I leave Fletcher alone in my *store*. . . . He could take me off any time, day and night.

What are you telling me, Walt? This is nothing but poison, I don't want to hear it. *(Pause.)*

TEACH: And that is what you say.

DON: Yes. It is.

Pause.

TEACH: Think back, Donny. Last night. On one hand. You lost
two hundred bucks.

Pause.

You got the straight, you stand pat. I go down before the
draw.

DON: Yeah.

TEACH: He's got what?

DON: A flush.

TEACH: That is correct. How many did he take?

DON: What?

TEACH: How many did he take?

Pause.

DON: One?

TEACH: No. Two, Don. He took two.

Pause.

DON: Yeah. He took two on that hand.

TEACH: He takes two on your standing pat, you kicked him
thirty bucks? He draws two, comes out with a *flush*?

DON *(Pause)*: Yeah?

TEACH: And spills his fucking Fresca?

DON: Yeah?

TEACH: Oh. You remember that?

DON *(Pause)*: Yeah.

TEACH: And we look down.

DON: Yeah.

TEACH: When we look back, he has come up with a king-high
flush.

Pause.

After he has drawed two.

Pause.

You're better than that, Don. You *knew* you had him beat, and you were right.

Pause.

DON: It could happen.

TEACH: Donny . . .

DON: Yeah?

TEACH: He laid down five red cards. A heart flush to the king.

Pause.

DON: Yeah?

TEACH: I swear to God as I am standing here that when I threw my hand in when you raised me out, that I folded the king of hearts.

Pause.

DON: You never called him out.

TEACH: No.

DON: How come?

TEACH: (He don't got the address the guy?)

DON: I told you he didn't.

Pause.

He's cheating, you couldn't say anything?

TEACH: It's not my responsibility, to cause bloodshed. I am not your keeper. You want to face facts, okay.

DON: I can't believe this, Teach.

TEACH: (Friendship is marvelous.)

DON: You couldn't say a word?

TEACH: I tell you now.

DON: He was cheating, you couldn't say anything?

TEACH: Don. Don, I see you're put out, you find out this guy is a cheat. . . .

DON: According to you.

TEACH: According to me, yes. I am the person it's usually according *to* when I'm talking. Have you noticed this? And I'm not crazed about it you're coming out I would lie to you on this. *Fuck* this. On anything. Wake up, Jim. I'm not the cheat. I know you're not mad at me, who are you mad at? Who fucked you up here, Don? Who's not here? Who?

DON: Ruth knows he cheats?

TEACH: Who is the bitch in league with?

DON: Him?

TEACH *(Pause)*: You know how much money they took from this game?

DON: Yeah?

TEACH: Well, I could be wrong.

DON: Don't fuck with me here, Teach.

TEACH: I don't fuck with my friends, Don. I don't fuck with my business associates. I am a businessman, I am here to do business, I am here to face facts.

(Will you open your eyes . . . ?) The kid comes in here, he has got a certain coin, it's like the one *you* used to have . . . the guy you brought in doesn't show, we don't know where *he* is.

Pause.

Something comes down, some guy gets his house took off.

Pause.

Fletcher, he's not showing up. All right. Let's say I don't know why. Let's say *you* don't know why. But I know that we're both better off. We are better off, Don.

Pause.

What time is it?

DON: It's midnight.

Pause.

TEACH: I'm going out there now. I'll need the address.

TEACH *takes out revolver and begins to load it.*

DON: What's that?

TEACH: What?

DON: That.

TEACH: This "gun"?

DON: Yes.

TEACH: What does it look like?

DON: A gun.

TEACH: It *is* a gun.

DON *(rises and crosses to center)*: I don't like it.

TEACH: Don't look at it.

DON: I'm serious.

TEACH: So am I.

DON: We don't need a gun, Teach.

TEACH: I pray that we don't, Don.

DON: We don't, tell me why we need a gun.

TEACH: It's not a question do we *need* it . . . *Need* . . . Only that it makes me comfortable, okay? It helps me to relax.

So, God forbid, something inevitable occurs and the choice is (And I'm *saying* "God forbid") it's either him or us.

DON: Who?

TEACH: The guy. I'm saying God forbid the *guy* (or somebody) comes in, he's got a knife . . . a cleaver from one of those magnetic *boards* . . . ?

DON: Yeah?

TEACH: . . . with the two *strips* . . . ?

DON: Yeah?

TEACH: And *whack,* and somebody is bleeding to death. This is all. Merely as a deterrent.

    Pause.

All the preparation in the world does not mean *shit,* the path of some crazed lunatic sees you as an invasion of his personal domain. Guys go nuts, Don, *you* know this. Public *officials* . . . Ax murderers . . . all I'm saying, look out for your own.

DON: I don't like the gun.

TEACH: It's a personal thing, Don. A personal thing of mine. A silly personal thing. I just like to have it along. Is this so unreasonable?

DON: I don't want it.

TEACH: I'm not going without it.

DON: Why do you want it?

TEACH: Protection of me and my partner. Protection, deterrence. (We're only going around the fucking *corner* for chrissake . . .)

DON: I don't want it with.

TEACH: I can't step down on this, Don. I got to have it with. The light of things as they are.

DON: Why?

TEACH: Because of the way *things* are. *(He looks out window.)* Hold on a second.

DON: Fletcher?

TEACH: Cops.

DON: What are they doing?

TEACH: Cruising.

    Pause.

DON: They turn the corner?

TEACH: Hold on.

Pause.

Yes.

They have the right idea. Armed to the hilt. Sticks, Mace, knives . . . who knows *what* the fuck they got. They have the right idea. Social customs break down, next thing *everybody's* lying in the gutter.

A knocking is heard at the door.

(Get down.) (Douse the light.)

DON: (Lemme see who it is . . .)

TEACH: Don't answer it.

BOB *(from behind door)*: Donny?

TEACH: (Great.)

DON: (It's Bobby.)

TEACH: (I know.)
BOB: Donny?

Pause.

TEACH: (Don't let him in.)

DON: (He knows we're in here.)

TEACH: (So let him go away, then.)

BOB: I got to talk to you.

DON *looks at* TEACH.

DON *(to* BOB*)*: What is it?

BOB: I can't come in?

TEACH: (Get him outta here.)

Pause.

DON: Bob . . .

BOB: Yeah?

DON: We're busy here.

BOB: I got to talk to you.

> DON *looks at* TEACH.

TEACH: (Is he alone?)

DON: (I think.)

TEACH *(Pause)*: (Hold on.)

> TEACH *opens door and pulls* BOB *in.*

What, Bob? What do you want? You know we got work to do here, we don't need you to do it, so what are you doing here and what do you want?

BOB: To talk to Don.

TEACH: Well, Don does not want to talk to you.

BOB: I *got* to talk to him.

TEACH: You do not have to do anything, Bob. You do not have to do anything that we tell you that you have to do.

BOB: I got to talk to Donny. *(To* DON*)* Can I talk to you? *(Pause. To* DON.*)* I came here . . .

DON: . . . yeah?

BOB: . . . The Riverside?

DON: Yeah?

BOB: Grace and Ruthie . . . he's in the hospital. Fletch·

> *Pause.*

I only wanted to, like, *come* here. I know you guys are only playing *cards* this . . . now. I didn't want to disturb you like *up,* but they just I found out he was in the hospital and I came over here to . . . tell you.

> *Pause.*

TEACH: With what?

BOB: He got mugged.

TEACH: You're so full of shit.

BOB: I think some Mexicans.

TEACH *snorts.*

He did. He's in the hospital.

TEACH: You see this, Don?

DON: He's mugged?

BOB: Yeah, Grace, they just got back. They broke his jaw.

TEACH: They broke his jaw.

BOB: Yeah. Broke.

TEACH: And now he's in the hospital. Grace and Ruthie just got back. You thought that you'd come over.

BOB: Yeah.

TEACH: Well, how about this, Don? Here Fletch is in Masonic Hospital a needle in his arm, huh. How about this?

DON: How bad is he?

BOB: They broke his jaw.

DON: What else?

BOB: I don't know.

TEACH: Would you believe this if I told you this this afternoon?

DON: When did it happen, Bob?

BOB: Like before.

DON: Before, huh?

BOB: Yeah.

TEACH: How about this, Don?

BOB: We're going to see him tomorrow.

DON: When?

BOB: I don't know. In the morning.

DON: They got hours in the morning?

BOB: I guess so.

TEACH: Hey, thanks for coming here. You did real good in coming here.

BOB: Yeah?

TEACH *(to* DON*)*: He did real good in coming here, huh, Donny? *(To* BOB*)* We really owe you something.

BOB: What for?

TEACH: Coming here.

BOB: What?

TEACH: Something.

BOB: Like what?

DON: He don't know. He's saying that he thinks we owe you something, but right now he can't think what it is.

BOB: Thanks, Teach.

TEACH: It's okay, Bob.

> *Pause.* BOB *starts to exit.*

Stick around.

BOB: Okay. For a minute.

TEACH: What? You're busy?

BOB: I got, like, some things to do.

TEACH: Whaddaya got, a "date"?

BOB: No.

TEACH: What, then?

BOB: Business.

> *Pause.*

DON: Where did they take him, Bob?

> *Pause.*

BOB: Uh, Masonic.

DON: I don't think that they got hours start til after lunch.

BOB: Then we'll go then. I'm gonna go now.

TEACH: Hold on a second, Bob. I feel we should take care of you for coming here.

BOB: That's okay. I'll see you guys.

DON: Come here a minute, Bobby.

BOB: What, Donny?

DON: What's going on here?

BOB: Here?

DON: Yes.

    Pause.

BOB: Nothing.

DON: I'm saying what's happening, Bob?

BOB: I don't know.

DON: Where did you get that nickel from?

BOB: What nickel?

DON: You know what nickel, Bob, the nickel I'm talking about.

BOB: I got it off a guy.

DON: What guy?

BOB: I met downtown.

TEACH: What was he wearing?

BOB: Things.

    Pause.

DON: How'd you get it off him, Bob?

BOB: We kinda talked.

    Pause.

DON: You know what, you look funny, Bob.

BOB: I'm late.

DON: It's after midnight, Bob. What are you late for?

BOB: Nothing.

DON *(very sadly)*: Jesus. Are you fucking with me here?

BOB: No.

DON: (Bobby.)

BOB: I'm not fucking with you, Donny.

> *Pause.*

DON: Where's Fletcher?

> *Pause.*

BOB: Masonic.

> DON *goes to telephone and dials information.*

DON *(into phone)*: For Masonic Hospital, please.

BOB: . . . I *think* . . .

DON *(to* BOB*)*: What?

BOB: He might not be Masonic.

DON *(to phone)*: Thank you. *(Hangs up phone. To* BOB*)* Now, *what?*

BOB: He might not *be* there . . .

DON: You said he was there.

BOB: Yeah, I just, like, I *said* it. I really don't remember what they said, Ruthie.

TEACH: (Ruthie.)

BOB: . . . so I just . . . *said* Masonic.

DON: Why?

BOB: I thought of it.

> *Pause.*

DON: Uh-huh. *(To phone)* Yes. I'm looking for a guy was just admitted. Fletcher Post.

> *Pause.*

Just a short time ago.

> *Pause.*

Thank you. *(Pause. To* BOB *and* TEACH*)* She's looking for it. *(To phone)* No?

BOB: (I told you . . .)

DON: You're sure?

>*Pause.*

Thank you. *(Hangs up phone. To* BOB*)* He's not there.

BOB: I told you.

TEACH: (What did I tell you, Don?)

DON: Where is he?

BOB: Somewhere else.

DON: (This makes me nuts . . .) Bobby . . .

BOB: Yeah?

>*Pause.*

They broke his jaw.

DON: Who?

BOB: Some spics. I don't know.

>TEACH *snorts.*

They did.

DON: Who?

TEACH: Yeah.

DON: Who is this "they," Bob, that you're talking about?

TEACH: Bob. . . .

BOB: . . . yeah?

TEACH: Who are these people you're talking about?

BOB: They broke his jaw.

TEACH: They took it in them all of a sudden they broke his jaw.

BOB: They didn't care it was him.

TEACH: No?

BOB: No, Teach.

TEACH: So who is it takes him out by accident. Huh? Grace and Ruthie?

BOB: They wouldn't do that.

TEACH: I'm not saying they would.

BOB *(to* DON*)*: What is he saying, Donny?

TEACH: Bob, Bob, Bob . . . what am I saying . . .

> *Pause.*

DON: Where's Fletch, Bobby?

BOB: Hospital.

TEACH: Aside from that.

BOB: All I know, that's the only place he is, Teach.

TEACH: Now, don't get smart with me, Bob, don't get smart with me, you young fuck, we've been sweating blood all day on this and I don't want your smart mouth on it (fuck around with Grace and Ruthie, and you come in here . . .), so all we want some answers. Do you understand?

> *Pause.*

I told you: Do you understand this?

DON: You better answer him.

BOB: I understand.

TEACH: Then let's make *this* clear: Loyalty does not mean *shit* a situation like this; I don't know what you and them are up to, and I do not *care,* but only you come clean with us.

BOB: He might of been a different hospital.

TEACH: Which one?

BOB: *Any* of 'em.

DON: So why'd you say "Masonic"?

BOB: I just thought of it.

TEACH: Okay. Okay. . . . Bob?

BOB: . . . yes?

TEACH: I want for you to tell us here and now (and for your own protection) what is going *on*, what is set *up* . . . where *Fletcher* is . . . and everything you know.

DON *(sotto voce)*:   (I can't believe this.)

BOB: I don't know anything.

TEACH: You don't, huh?

BOB: No.

DON: Tell him what you know, Bob.

BOB: I don't know it, Donny. Grace and Ruthie . . .

> TEACH *grabs a nearby object and hits* BOB *viciously on the side of the head.*

TEACH: Grace and Ruthie up your ass, you shithead; you don't fuck with us, *I'll* kick your fucking head in. (I don't give a shit . . .)

> *Pause.*

You *twerp* . . .

> *A pause near the end of which* BOB *starts whimpering.*

I don't give a shit. (Come in here with your fucking stories . . .)

> *Pause.*

Imaginary people in the hospital . . .

> BOB *starts to cry.*

That don't mean shit to me, you fruit.

BOB: Donny . . .

DON: You brought it on yourself.

TEACH: Sending us out there . . . who the fuck knows what . .

BOB: He's in the hospital.

DON: Which hospital?

BOB: I don't know.

TEACH: Well, then, you better make one up, and quick.

DON: Bob . . .

TEACH: (Don't back down on this, Don. Don't back down on me, here.)

DON: Bob . . .

BOB: . . . yeah?

DON: You got to see our point here.

BOB *(whimpering)*: Yeah, I do.

DON: Now, we don't want to hit you . . .

TEACH: (No.)

BOB: I know you don't.

TEACH: No.

DON: But you come in here . . .

BOB: . . . yeah . . .

DON: . . . the only one who knows the score . . .

BOB: Yeah . . . (My ear is bleeding. It's coming out my ear.) Oh, fuck, I'm real scared.

DON: (Shit.)

BOB: I don't feel good.

TEACH: (Fuckin' kid poops out on us . . .)

BOB: Don . . .

TEACH: Now what are we going to do with this?

DON: You know, we didn't want to do this to you, Bob.

BOB: I know . . .

DON: We didn't want to do this.

    Phone rings.

TEACH: (Great.)

DON *(to phone)*: What? What the fuck do *you* want?

TEACH: (It's the guy?)

DON: (It's Ruthie.) *(To phone)* Oh yeah, we heard about that, Ruth.

TEACH: *(She's* got a lot of nerve . . .)

DON *(to phone)*: From Bobby. Yeah. We'll *all* go.

Pause.

I thought he was at Masonic? Bobby. Well, okay, that's where we'll go then, Ruthie, we aren't going to go and see him at some hospital he isn't even *at* . . .

Pause.

Bobby's not here. I will. Okay. I will. Around eleven. Okay. *(He hangs up.)*

TEACH *(to* BOB*)*: And you owe me twenty bucks.

DON *(dialing)*: For Columbus Hospital, please.

TEACH: (Fuckin' medical costs . . .)

DON: Thank you.

TEACH *(singing softly to himself)*: ". . . and I'm never ever sick at sea."

DON: Yes. For Fletcher Post, please, he was just admitted?

Pause.

No. I only want to know is he all right, and when we go to see him.

Pause.

Thank you.

TEACH: What?

DON: She's looking. *(To phone)* Yes? Yeah. Thank you very much. Yes. You've been very kind. *(He hangs up phone.)*

TEACH: What is he, *in* there?

DON: Yeah.

TEACH: And they won't let us talk to him?

DON: His jaw is broke.

BOB: I feel funny.

TEACH: Your *ear* hurts.

DON: Bob, it hurts. Bob?

TEACH: I never felt quite right on this.

DON: Go tilt your head the other way.

TEACH I mean, we're fucked up here. We have not blown the shot, but we're fucked up.

DON: We are going to take you to the hospital.

TEACH: Yeah, yeah, we'll take you to the hospital, you'll get some *care,* this isn't a big deal.

DON: Bob, you fell downstairs, you hurt your ear.

TEACH: He understands?

DON: You understand? We're going to take you to the hospital, you fell downstairs.

TEACH *(at door)*: This fucking rain.

DON: You give 'em your right name, Bob, and you know what you can tell 'em. *(Reaches in pocket, thrusts money at* BOB.*)* You hold on to this, Bob. Anything you want inside the hospital.

BOB: I don't want to go to the hospital.

TEACH: You're going to the hospital, and that's the end of it.

BOB: I don't want to.

DON: You got to, Bob.

BOB: Why?

TEACH: You're fucked up, that's why.

BOB: I'm gonna do the job.

DON: We aren't going to do the job tonight, Bob.

TEACH: You got a hat or something keep my head dry?

DON: No.

BOB: I get to do the job.

TEACH: You shut up. You are going in the hospital.

DON: We aren't going to do the job tonight.

BOB: We do it sometime else.

DON: Yeah.

TEACH: He ain't going to do no job.

DON: Shut up.

TEACH: Just say he isn't going to do no job.

DON: It's done now.

TEACH: What?

DON: I'm saying, this is over.

TEACH: No, it's not, Don. It is not. He does no job.

DON: You leave the fucking kid alone.

TEACH: You want kids, you go have them. *I* am not your wife. *This* doesn't mean a thing to me. *I'm* in this. And it *isn't* over. This is for me, and this is my question:

   Pause.

Where did you get that coin?

BOB: What?

TEACH: Where'd you get that fucking nickel, if it all comes out now.

   Pause.

He comes in here, a fifty dollars for a nickel, where'd you get it?

BOB: Take me to the hospital.

   Pause.

TEACH: Where did you get that nickel? (I want you to watch this.)

Pause.

BOB: I bought it.

TEACH: (Mother Fucking Junkies.)

DON: Shut up.

TEACH: What are you saying that you bought that coin?

BOB: Yeah.

TEACH: Where?

BOB: A coin store.

    Pause.

TEACH: You bought it in a coin store.

BOB: Yeah.

    Pause.

TEACH: Why?

DON: Go get your car.

TEACH: What did you pay for it?

    Pause.

What did you pay for it?

BOB: Fifty dollars.

TEACH: You buy a coin for fifty dollars, you come back here.

    Pause.

Why?

DON: Go get your fucking car.

TEACH: Why would you do a thing like that?

BOB: I don't know.

TEACH: Why would you go do a thing like that?

BOB: For Donny.

    Pause.

TEACH: You people make my flesh crawl.

DON: Bob, we're going to take you out of here.

TEACH: I can not take this anymore.

DON: Can you walk?

BOB: No.

DON: Go and get your car.

TEACH: I am not your nigger. I am not your wife.

DON: I'm through with you today.

TEACH: You are.

DON: Yes.

TEACH: Why?

     Pause.

DON: You have lamed this up real good.

TEACH: I did.

DON: Real good.

TEACH: I lamed it up.

BOB: He hit me.

DON: I know, Bob.

TEACH: Yes, I hit him. For his own good. For the good of all.

DON: Get out of here.

TEACH: "Get out of here"? And now you throw me out like *trash?* I'm doing this for *you.* What do I have to wreck this joint *apart?* He told you that he bought it in a *coin store.*

DON: I don't care.

TEACH: You don't *care?* (I cannot believe this.) You *believe* him?

DON: I don't *care.* I don't *care* anymore.

TEACH: You *fake.* You fucking *fake.* You fuck your friends. You *have* no friends. No *wonder* that you fuck this kid around.

DON: You shut your mouth.

TEACH: You seek your friends with *junkies.* You're a joke on this street, you and him.

DON: Get out.

TEACH: I do not go out, no.

BOB: (I eat shit.)

DON: You get out of here.

TEACH: I am not going anywhere. I have a piece of this.

DON: You have a piece of *shit,* you fucking lame. *(Advancing on him.)*

TEACH: (This from a man who has to buy his friends.)

DON: *I'll* tell you friends, *I'll* give you friends . . . (Still advancing.)

BOB: (Oh, fuck . . .)

DON: The stinking deals you come in here . . .

TEACH: You stay away from me . . .

DON: You stiff this one, you stiff that one . . . you come in here, you stick this poison in me . . . *(hitting him).*

TEACH: (Oh, Christ . . .)

BOB: (I eat shit.)

TEACH: (Oh, my God, I live with madmen.)

DON: All these years . . .

BOB: (A cause I missed him.)

DON *(advancing again)*: All these fucking years . . .

TEACH: (You're going to hit me.)

BOB: Donny . . .

DON: You make life of garbage.

BOB: Donny!

TEACH: (Oh, my God.)

BOB: I missed him.

DON *(stopping)*: What?

BOB: I got to tell you what a fuck I am.

DON: What?

BOB: I missed him.

DON: Who?

BOB: The guy.

DON: What guy?

BOB: The guy this morning.

DON: What guy?

BOB: With the suitcase.

DON *(Pause)*: You missed him?

BOB: I eat shit.

DON: What are you saying that you lied to me?

BOB: I eat shit.

TEACH: What is he saying?

  Pause.

DON: You're saying that you lied?

TEACH: What is he saying?

DON: You're saying you didn't see him with the suitcase?

TEACH: This kid is hysterical.

DON: You didn't see him?

TEACH: He's saying that he didn't see him?

DON: When he left this morning.

TEACH: He's saying that he lied?

BOB: I'm going to throw up.

TEACH: He's saying he didn't see the guy?

  Pause.

When he came out. I was in here. *Then* you saw him. When he had the suitcase. *(Pause.)* Then.

> *Pause.*

You saw him *then*.

> *Pause.* BOB *shakes his head.*

My Whole Cocksucking Life.

> TEACH *picks up the dead-pig sticker and starts trashing the junkshop.*

The Whole Entire World.

There Is No Law.

There Is No Right And Wrong.

The World Is Lies.

There Is No Friendship.

Every Fucking Thing.

> *Pause.*

Every God-forsaken Thing.

DON: Calm down, Walt.

TEACH: We all live like the cavemen.

> *During the speech,* DON *tries to subdue* TEACH, *and finally does.*

DON: (Siddown.)

> *Pause.*

> TEACH *sits still.*

TEACH: I went on a limb for you.

> *Pause.*

You don't know what I go through. I put my dick on the chopping block.

> *Pause.*

I hock my fucking watch . . .

> *Pause.*

I go out there. I'm out there every day.

Pause.

There is nothing out there.

Pause.

I fuck myself.

Pause.

DON: Are you all right?

TEACH: What?

DON: Are you all right.

TEACH: How the fuck do I know?

DON: You tire me out, Walt.

TEACH: What?

DON: I need a rest.

TEACH: This fucking day.

DON *(Pause)*: My shop's fucked up.

TEACH: I know.

DON: It's all fucked up.

Pause.

You fucked my shop up.

TEACH: Are you mad at me?

DON: What?

TEACH: Are you mad at me?

Pause.

DON: Come on.

TEACH: Are you?

DON: Go and get your car. Bob?

TEACH *(Pause)*: Tell me are you mad at me.

DON: No.

TEACH: You aren't?

DON: No.

Pause.

TEACH: Good.

DON: You go and get your car.

TEACH: You got a hat?

DON: No.

TEACH: Do you have a piece of paper?

DON: Bob . . . ?

TEACH walks to counter, takes a piece of newspaper, and starts making himself a paper hat.

TEACH: He's all right?

DON: Bob . . . ?

TEACH: Is he all right?

DON: Bob . . . ?

BOB *(waking up)*: What?

DON: Come on. We're taking you the hospital.

TEACH puts on paper hat and looks at self in window.

TEACH: I look like a sissy.

DON: Go and get your car.

Pause.

TEACH: Can you get him to the door?

DON: Yeah.

Pause.

TEACH: I'm going to get my car.

DON: You gonna honk?

TEACH: Yeah.

DON: Good.

TEACH: I'll honk the horn.

Pause.

DON: Good.

    Pause.

TEACH: This fucking day, huh?

DON: Yeah.

TEACH: I know it. You should clean this place up.

DON: Yeah.

    Pause.

TEACH: Good. *(Exits.)*

DON: Bob.

BOB: What?

DON: Get up.

    Pause.

  Bob. I'm sorry.

BOB: What?

DON: I'm sorry.

BOB: I fucked up.

DON: No. You did real good.

BOB: No.

DON: Yeah. You did real good.

    Pause.

BOB: Thank you.

DON: That's all right.

    Pause.

BOB: I'm sorry, Donny.

DON: That's all right.

    Lights dim.

Selected List of Grove Press Drama and Theater Paperbacks

E487   ABE, KOBE / Friends / $2.45
E449   ARDEN, JOHN / Armstrong's Last Goodnight / $1.50
E412   ARDEN, JOHN / The Business of Good Government: A Christmas Play / $1.45
E404   ARDEN, JOHN / Left-Handed Liberty: A Play About Magna Carta / $2.45
E312   ARDEN, JOHN / Serjeant Musgrave's Dance / $2.45 [See also Modern British Drama, Henry Popkin, ed. GT614 / $5.95]
B109   ARDEN, JOHN / Three Plays: Live Like Pigs, The Waters of Babylon, The Happy Haven / $2.45
E610   ARRABAL, FERNANDO / And They Put Handcuffs on The Flowers / $1.95
E486   ARRABAL, FERNANDO / The Architect and The Emperor of Assyria / $2.40
E611   ARRABAL, FERNANDO / Garden of Delights / $2.95
E521   ARRABAL, FERNANDO / Guernica and Other Plays (The Labyrinth, The Tricycle, Picnic on the Battlefield) / $2.45
E532   ARTAUD, ANTONIN / The Cenci / $1.95
E127   ARTAUD, ANTONIN / The Theater and Its Double (Critical Study) / $2.95
E425   BARAKA, IMAMU AMIRI (LEROI JONES) / The Baptism and The Toilet / $2.45
E540   BARNES, PETER / The Ruling Class / $2.95
E471   BECKETT, SAMUEL / Cascando and Other Short Dramatic Pieces (Words and Music, Film, Play, Come and Go, Eh Joe, Endgame) / $1.95
E96   BECKETT, SAMUEL / Endgame / $1.95
E318   BECKETT, SAMUEL / Happy Days / $2.45
E226   BECKETT, SAMUEL / Krapp's Last Tape, plus All That Fall, Embers, Act Without Words I and II / $2.45
E33   BECKETT, SAMUEL / Waiting For Godot / $1.95 [See also Seven Plays of the Modern Theater, Harold Clurman, ed. GT422 / $4.95]
B79   BEHAN, BRENDAN / The Quare Fellow* and The Hostage**: Two Plays / $2.45 *[See also Seven Plays of the Modern Theater, Harold Clurman, ed. GT422 / $4.95] **[See also Modern British Drama, Henry Popkin, ed. GT614 / $5.95]

E624	BEHAN, BRENDAN / Richard's Cork Leg / $2.95
E534	BENTLEY, ERIC / A Time to Die and A Time to Live: Two Short Plays / $1.95
GT423	BOWERS, FAUBIAN / Theatre in the East: A Survey of Asian Dance and Drama / $3.95
B117	BRECHT, BERTOLT / The Good Woman of Setzuan / $1.95
B80	BRECHT, BERTOLT / The Jewish Wife and Other Short Plays (In Search of Justice, The Informer, The Elephant Calf, The Measures Taken, The Exception and the Rule, Salzburg Dance of Death) / $1.65
B90	BRECHT, BERTOLT / The Mother / $1.45
B108	BRECHT, BERTOLT / Mother Courage and Her Children / $1.50
B333	BRECHT, BERTOLT / The Threepenny Opera / $1.45
B88	BRECHT, BERTOLT / The Visions of Simone Machard / $1.25
E517	BULGAKOV, MIKHAIL / Flight: A Play in Eight Dreams and Four Acts / $2.25
E520	COE, RICHARD N. (Ed.) / The Theater of Jean Genet: A Casebook / $3.95
E441	COHN, RUBY (Ed.) / Casebook on Waiting for Godot / $3.95
E581	CESAIRE, AIME / A Season in the Congo / $2.45
GT422	CLURMAN, HAROLD (Ed.) / Seven Plays of the Modern Theater / $4.95 (Waiting For Godot by Samuel Beckett, The Quare Fellow by Brendan Behan, A Taste of Honey by Shelagh Delaney, The Connection by Jack Gelber, The Balcony by Jean Genet, Rhinoceros by Eugene Ionesco, and The Birthday Party by Harold Pinter)
E159	DELANEY, SHELAGH / A Taste of Honey / $1.95 (See also Modern British Drama, Henry Popkin, ed., GT614 / $5.95, and Seven Plays of the Modern Theater, Harold Clurman, ed. GT422 / $4.95)
E402	DURRENMATT, FRIEDRICH / An Angel Comes to Babylon and Romulus the Great / $3.95
E401	DURRENMATT, FRIEDRICH / The Marriage of Mr. Mississippi and Problems of the Theatre (Play and Essay) / $3.95
E628	DURRENMATT, FRIEDRICH / The Meteor / $1.95
E380	DURRENMATT, FRIEDRICH / The Physicists / $2.95

E612	DURRENMATT, FRIEDRICH / Play Strindberg / $1.95
E344	DURRENMATT, FRIEDRICH / The Visit / $2.75
B215	DYER, CHARLES / Staircase / $1.95
B132	GARSON, BARBARA / MacBird! / $1.95
E223	GELBER, JACK / The Connection / $2.45 [See also Seven Plays of the Modern Theater, Harold Clurman, ed. GT422 / $4.95]
E130	GENET, JEAN / The Balcony / $2.95 [See also Seven Plays of the Modern Theater, Harold Clurman, ed. GT422 / $4.95]
E208	GENET, JEAN / The Blacks: A Clown Show / $2.95
E479	GENET, JEAN / Letters to Roger Blin / $1.95
E577	GENET, JEAN / The Maids and Deathwatch: Two Plays / $2.95
E374	GENET, JEAN / The Screens / $1.95
E482	GOMBROWICZ, WITOLD / The Marriage / $1.95
E451	GOMBROWICZ, WITOLD / Ivona, Princess of Burgundia / $1.95
E484	GUARE, JOHN / Cop Out, Muzeeka,* Home Fires / $1.95 *[See also Showcase I: Plays from the O'Neill Foundation, John Lahr, ed. B233 / $1.95]
E615	HARRISON, PAUL CARTER (Ed.) / The Kuntu Drama / $4.95 (Kabnis by Jean Toomer, A Season in the Congo by Aime Cesaire, The Owl Answers and A Beast Story by Adrienne Kennedy, Great Goodness of Life by Imamu Amiri Baraka (LeRoi Jones), Devil Mas' by Lennox Brown, The Sty of the Blind Pig by Phillip Hayes Dean, Mars By Clay Goss, The Great MacDaddy by Paul Carter Harrison)
E457	HERBERT, JOHN / Fortune and Men's Eyes / $2.95
B154	HOCHHUTH, ROLF / The Deputy / $2.95
B200	HOCHHUTH, ROLF / Soldiers / $1.50
E427	HOFMANN, GERT / The Burgomaster / $1.50
E456	IONESCO, EUGENE / Exit the King / $2.95
E101	IONESCO, EUGENE / Four Plays (The Bald Soprano, The Lesson, The Chairs,* Jack, or The Submission) / $1.95 *[See also Eleven Short Plays of the Modern Theater, Samuel Moon, ed. B107 / $2.45]
E646	IONESCO, EUGENE / A Hell of a Mess / $3.95
E506	IONESCO, EUGENE / Hunger and Thirst and Other Plays / $1.95

E189   IONESCO, EUGENE / The Killer and Other Plays (Improvisation, or The Shepherd's Chameleon, Maid to Marry) / $2.45

E613   IONESCO, EUGENE / Killing Game / $1.95

E259   IONESCO, EUGENE / Rhinoceros* and Other Plays (The Leader, The Future is in Eggs, or It Takes All Sorts to Make a World) / $1.95 *[See also Seven Plays of the Modern Theater, Harold Clurman, ed. GT422 / $4.95]

E485   IONESCO, EUGENE / A Stroll in the Air and Frenzy for Two: Two Plays / $2.45

E119   IONESCO, EUGENE / Three Plays (Amédée, The New Tenant, Victims of Duty) / $2.95

E387   IONESCO, EUGENE / Notes and Counter Notes / $3.95

E496   JARRY, ALFRED / The Ubu Plays / $2.95

E443   JELLICOE, ANNE / Shelley, or The Idealist / $1.50

E633   LAHR, JOHN (Ed.) / Grove Press Modern Drama / $6.95 (The Caucasian Chalk Circle by Bertolt Brecht, The Toilet by Imamu Amiri Baraka (LeRoi Jones), The White House Murder Case by Jules Feiffer, The Blacks by Jean Genet, Rhinoceros by Eugene Ionesco, Tango by Slawomir Mrozek)

B233   LAHR, JOHN (Ed.) / Showcase I: Plays from the Eugene O'Neill Foundation / $1.95 (Who's Happy Now by Oliver Hailey, The Indian Wants the Bronx by Israel Horovitz, Father Uxbridge Wants to Marry by Frank Gagliano, Muzeeka by John Guare)

E545   LAHR, JOHN / Up Against the Fourth Wall: Essays on Modern Theater / $2.95

B142   McCLURE, MICHAEL / The Beard / $1.25

B107   MOON, SAMUEL (Ed.) / One Act: Eleven Short Plays of the Modern Theater / $2.45 (Miss Julie by August Strindberg, Purgatory by William Butler Yeats, The Man With the Flower in His Mouth by Luigi Pirandello, Pullman Car Hiawatha by Thornton Wilder, Hello Out There by William Saroyan, 27 Wagons Full of Cotton by Tennessee Williams, Bedtime Story by Sean O'Casey, Cecile by Jean Anouilh, This Music Crept by Me Upon the Waters by Archibald MacLeish, A Memory of Two Mondays by Arthur Miller, The Chairs by Eugene Ionesco)

E410   MROZEK, SLAWOMIR / Six Plays: The Police, Out at Sea, Enchanted Night, The Party, Charlie, The Martyrdom of Peter Ohey / $2.45

E433   MROZEK, SLAWOMIR / Tango / $1.95

E568   MROZEK, SLAWOMIR / Vatzlav / $1.95

E462   NICHOLS, PETER / Joe Egg / $2.95

E650   NICHOLS, PETER / The National Health / $3.95

E393   ORTON, JOE / Entertaining Mr. Sloane / $2.95

E470   ORTON, JOE / Loot / $1.95

E567   ORTON, JOE / What The Butler Saw / $2.40

E583   OSBORNE, JOHN / Inadmissible Evidence / $2.45

B110   OSBORNE, JOHN / Plays for England and The World of Paul Slickey / $1.45 (The Blood of the Bambergs and Under Plain Cover)

B354   PINTER, HAROLD / Old Times / $1.95

E315   PINTER, HAROLD / The Birthday Party* and The Room: Two Plays / $1.95 *[See also Seven Plays of the Modern Theater, Harold Clurman, ed. GT422 / $4.95]

E299   PINTER, HAROLD / The Caretaker* and The Dumb Waiter: Two Plays / $1.95 *[See also Modern British Drama, Henry Popkin, ed. GT422 / $5.95]

E411   PINTER, HAROLD / The Homecoming / $1.95

E432   PINTER, HAROLD / The Lover, Tea Party, The Basement: Three Plays / $1.95

E480   PINTER, HAROLD / A Night Out, Night School, Revue Sketches: Early Plays / $1.95

GT614   POPKIN, HENRY (Ed.) / Modern British Drama / $5.95 (A Taste of Honey by Shelagh Delaney, The Hostage by Brendan Behan, Roots by Arnold Wesker, Serjeant Musgrave's Dance by John Arden, One Way Pendulum by N. F. Simpson, The Caretaker by Harold Pinter)

E538   ROSEWICZ, TADEUSZ / The Card Index and Other Plays / $1.95

E635   SHEPARD, SAM / The Tooth of Crime and Geography of a Horsedreamer / $3.95

E626   STOPPARD, TOM / Jumpers / $1.95

B319   STOPPARD, TOM / Rosencrantz and Guilderstern Are Dead / $1.95

E660   STOREY, DAVID / In Celebration / $2.95

B212   TUOTTI, JOSEPH D. / Big Time Buck White / $1.25
E434   VIAN, BORIS / The Generals' Tea Party / $1.95
E414   VIAN, BORIS / The Empire Builders / $2.95
E458   VIAN, BORIS / The Knacker's ABC / $1.95
E62   WALEY, ARTHUR (Translator) / The No Plays of
       Japan / $3.95
E519   WOOD, CHARLES / Dingo / $1.95

Critical Studies

E127   ARTAUD, ANTONIN / The Theater and Its Double / $2.95
GT423 BOWERS, FAUBIAN / Theatre in the East: A Survey of
       Asian Dance and Drama / $3.95
E520   COE, RICHARD N. (Ed.) / The Theater of Jean Genet:
       A Casebook / $3.95
E441   COHN, RUBY (Ed.) / Casebook on Waiting for
       Godot / $3.95
E479   GENET, JEAN / Letters to Roger Blin / $1.95
E387   IONESCO, EUGENE / Notes and Counter Notes / $3.95
E545   LAHR, JOHN / Up Against the Fourth Wall: Essays on
       Modern Theater / $2.95

GROVE PRESS, INC., 196 West Houston St., New York, N.Y. 10014